COUNTRIES
OF THE MIND

COUNTRIES OF THE MIND

ESSAYS IN LITERARY CRITICISM

By

JOHN MIDDLETON MURRY

FIRST SERIES

Essay Index Reprint Series

NEW EDITION, REVISED AND ENLARGED

Originally published by:

OXFORD UNIVERSITY PRESS

BOOKS FOR LIBRARIES PRESS, INC.
FREEPORT, NEW YORK

First Published 1931
Reprinted 1968

indexed in EGhl

LIBRARY OF CONGRESS CATALOG CARD NUMBER:

68-22111

Prefatory Note

TO THE FIRST EDITION (1922)

THE majority of these essays originally appeared in *The Times Literary Supplement*; others in the *Nation and Athenaeum*, the *London Mercury*, the *Dial*, and the *New Republic*. I have to thank the editors of these periodicals for permission to reprint them.

Many of them were written on the occasion of anniversaries. There is something arbitrary, therefore, in grouping them in a single volume; and yet perhaps their association is not really quite so accidental as may at first sight appear. The year 1821, in which Dostoevsky, Baudelaire, Flaubert, and Amiel were born, was obviously a crucial moment in the spiritual history of the nineteenth century; and these four men, animated by a similar spirit of disillusion, are best understood in relation to one another. Dostoevsky, it is true, is treated only incidentally in this volume: but I may be allowed to refer the reader to my earlier book, *Fyodor Dostoevsky: A Critical Study*.

The two essays on Shakespeare, the one as general as the other is particular, deal with what is essentially the same subject; while the two essays on Clare and Collins are complementary, as exhibiting two directly contrasted types of poetic sensibility.

Underlying all the essays in this volume is a theory of the psychology of literary creation, which is expounded in greater detail in a series of lectures on 'The Problem of Style', recently published. A few shorter essays are included, either because they are examples of the application of this theory or because they make clear my conviction that a theory of this kind, whether mine or another, is necessary to literary criticism, if it is not to be incoherent and spasmodic.

Two objections were frequently made by reviewers to the volume of essays, *Aspects of Literature*, to which this is the successor: first, that the principles on which it was based were not more elaborately and philosophically expounded; second, that it contained relatively little criticism of contemporary writers. The answer to both these objections is the same. A professional critic is almost entirely at the mercy of occasion. There are many things he would like to do which he cannot afford to do; instead, he spends a great deal of his life writing brief criticisms in which he is forced to mutilate his own opinions, theories, and ideals. This condition of things may easily seem more deplorable than it actually is; for, though it is pleasant to dream of a time when the exhaustive discussion of literary theory and practice will find an eager and appreciative audience, when the critic's tacit assertion that fine books and fine poems are not produced every week will no longer be thought to prove that he is lacking in sympathy, or even in common human kindness, the fact remains that compulsion has produced far more good literary work of every kind than the unembarrassed pursuit of an artistic ideal has ever done. And though it would be extravagant to urge that the struggle against arbitrary limitations in which a modern critic is engaged is the same as that exhilarating contest with a stringent literary form which is the condition of some of the greatest triumphs of literature, the likeness between them is sufficient to enable the critic to feel that, on the whole, he gains more than he loses by the effort.

Note

For this edition I have corrected some mistakes and amended some sentences. With some passages I no longer agree, but I have let them stand; for it is impossible to tinker with the expression of an opinion which was sincerely held at the time it was expressed. In one or two cases I have made a short comment on these passages at the end of the book.

I have added to this volume an essay on the late Charles Doughty's poetry written for *The Times Literary Supplement* on the occasion of his death;. also a second and later essay on Amiel, *Amiel's Love Story*.

Contents

I

SHAKESPEARE AND LOVE

IN a very interesting essay recently published[1] Professor
Herford discusses Shakespeare's attitude to love and
marriage, and insists upon what he calls the profound
'normality' of the poet's conception of love. He points
out that love is but seldom the substantial theme of
Shakespeare's greater tragedies, and that Shakespeare
conceives it as a condition which, so far from inevitably
containing the seed of its own disruption, is so naturally
strong that it needs the invasion of an alien power to be
prevented from the bliss of perfect fulfilment. If we may
translate Shakespeare's idea of love into terms he would
certainly not himself have used, we may say, following
out Professor Herford's view, that Shakespeare instinc-
tively thought of love as a beneficent power in the
human world, which could be thwarted from its true
purpose only by forces foreign to itself. Professor Herford concludes:

'Shakespeare certainly did not, so far as we can judge,
regard sexual love (like some moderns) as either the clue
to human life or as in any way related to the structure of
the universe. But if instead of these abstract questions, we
ask whether any poet has united in a like degree veracious
appreciation of love in its existing conditions with apprehension of all its ideal possibilities, we shall not dispute
Shakespeare's place among the foremost of the poets of love.'

That is, in substance, a singularly just conclusion, and
yet, we think, it will strike a reader of Shakespeare as
a little cold. It would, perhaps, scarcely have occurred

---

[1] *Shakespeare's Treatment of Love and Marriage, and Other Essays,* by
C. H. HERFORD (London: Fisher Unwin), 1921.

to him that Shakespeare's place among the foremost of
the poets of love should be disputed; and it is not unlikely that his natural impulse would be to call Shakespeare the greatest love-poet of them all. For the love
of many other great poets, 'the love which moves the
sun and the other stars,' is a wonderful and mighty
power, but it is hardly love. It bears the name only by
a sublime analogy; it is no native of the earth.

But in Shakespeare love is not remote and celestial;
it is warm and human, and generation after generation
of men and women to whom the intellectual love of a
Dante, a Spinoza, or a Shelley would be an unintelli-
gible fantasy have recognized it as a reflection of something they had felt or might hope to feel. If we take
that which ninety-nine out of a hundred of all sorts and
conditions of men feel or dream or understand at the
word love, as the rough ore of the mysterious element,
and if we refine this to the utmost of our power, casting
nothing away that truly belongs to it, then of the
recognizable universal love which remains Shakespeare
is the pre-eminent poet. Nor is this love less ideal
because it has nothing of the abstract-metaphysical in
its composition, unless we are to hand over the word
'ideal' wholly to the mercies of the philosophers. Shakespeare's conception of love is ideal in the most humane
sense of the word, an enchanting and attainable perfection of the real.

Tradition, the popular voice, the judgement of the
critics are at one in regarding Shakespeare as the poet
of the earthly felicity of love. For this he was 'sweet'
and 'gentle' in his own day, as he is in ours. The
evidence of the plays is beyond all doubt. It is not a
question of scattered lines or single characters, but of
the general sentiment pervading all his plays: it cannot

be escaped; it is the very air we breathe in them. Yet in this there is something strange, something miraculous almost; for whatever may be our estimate of the precise value of the Sonnets as autobiography, it is impossible for any one but a briefed advocate to assert that they do not substantially contain the record of the poet's own disaster in love. That earthly felicity of love between man and woman which runs, with but a single moment of interruption, like a thread of gold through the work of Shakespeare the dramatist, would seem to be the one aspect of love of which knowledge was denied to Shakespeare the sonnetteer. He seems to have tasted only the despairs, the degradations and the bitternesses, even though it was he also who declared his faith in the loyalty of a true lover's heart.

> Love is not love
> Which alters when it alteration finds
> Nor bends with the remover to remove.

If we seek a simple explanation of the fact, we shall say, well knowing that we trespass against Signor Croce's canons of criticism, that the sonnets of tormented love belong to the moment when the golden thread in the plays is suddenly and unexpectedly snapped. We shall hold that the Sonnets represent an episode in Shakespeare's experience which caused a momentary but a complete overclouding of the reflection in the mirror of the plays. The episode passes and the reflection becomes calm and serene once more. The Sonnets give us, as it were, a year of Shakespeare's attitude to love; the plays give us a lifetime. In other words, even in this single matter of love, it is a mistaken effort to measure the plays by the Sonnets; what we have to do is to measure the Sonnets by the plays. If we do this the sonnets of

disastrous love seem to fall naturally into place in that
period of profound disturbance which is expressed in
Hamlet, in *Measure for Measure*, in *Troilus and Cressida*,
and in *All's Well that Ends Well*. No doubt this disturbance had its manifest reactions in realms of Shakespeare's
faith other than his faith in love; it may have been the
proximate cause of his greatest tragedies. But for these
we need not assume an origin in personal catastrophe.
Moreover, in the great tragic period Shakespeare's faith
in love has manifestly begun to reassert itself. We have
only to imagine *Antony and Cleopatra* written in the mood
of *Troilus and Cressida* to understand what Shakespeare
actually chose to do with a theme that would have lent
itself magnificently to all the bitterness of an outraged
heart.[1]

If we put aside the plays of this period of disturbance,
which ordinary readers and literary critics alike have
felt to be discordant with Shakespeare's work as a whole,
we discover pervading the rest an attitude to love which
all cynics and most critics have conspired to describe as
romantic. It is true that it appears to flower most
divinely in what we call the romantic comedies; but
that does not mean that the love portrayed in them is
romantic in essence. Classification of this kind is superficial and confusing. A poet uses the most convenient
plot as the foundation on which to build up the expression of his emotional attitude. The mere accident that
the plot contains improbable coincidences and enchanted islands cannot affect the substance of the
attitude expressed by its means. The romantic comedy
of one poet may be a trivial indulgence of the fancy,
while that of another is the flashing of a warm light into

[1] See note, p. 190.

the verity of the human soul. We have only to compare Shakespeare's comedy on the one hand with Beaumont and Fletcher's, and on the other with Ben Jonson's, to discover how far asunder they are in their poetic truth. The segregation of Shakespeare's comedies is misleading unless it is considered merely as the distinction of an aspect within the whole work of Shakespeare. The most immature of his comedies is nearer in spirit to the most perfect of his tragedies than it is to the comedies of Jonson or Fletcher, whatever merits of their own these may possess.

To call the love of Shakespeare's romantic comedies itself romantic is meaningless, or it is the expression of a private and personal conviction concerning the nature of love. It may mean that in the opinion of the judge love is not in fact so happy, nor so secure, nor so deeply irradiated with the heart's delight as Shakespeare represented it; but it can mean nothing more. And we cannot tell whether Shakespeare himself believed that love actually was as he chose to represent it. But we can say that he did believe either that it was so, or that it ought to be so; and that he found it natural to create men and women who are alive with a reality no other created characters possess, who love in the way he chose to make them love, with a tenderness and a gaiety, an open-eyed confidence in themselves and the future, a shyness and a humour, a marvellous equality in affection, which have made them for a whole world of mankind the embodiment of their experience if they were happy in love, or of their dreams if they were disappointed. And this love, which is as solid and as ethereal, as earthly and as magical as a rose in full bloom, is in all his early comedies; it is essentially the same in *A Midsummer Night's Dream* as in *Much Ado about Nothing*. We can hardly say more than that the light changes from moon-light to full sunshine as we pass from Lysander and Hermia, through Orsino and Viola, to Benedick and Beatrice, and that when we reach *As You Like It* the mid-day brightness is faintly mellowed with afternoon. Nor is it possible to say that the love of the *Merchant of Venice* or of *Romeo and Juliet* is of another kind, though the one is calm and the other tempestuous. It is only the tempest of circumstance which wrecks the love of Romeo and Juliet. There is a peculiar ecstasy in their surrender to the enchantment, which bursts out like a flame at the clash of contact between the enemy houses; but in their love no seed of disruption or decay is visible, much less of disaster. Theirs is a love of which all human foresight could prophesy its

> Outliving beauty's outward with a mind
> That doth renew swifter than blood decays.

They are the victims not of their passion but of crass casualty; they are the fools of fortune, not themselves. *Romeo and Juliet*, as Professor Herford truly says, 'appears not to be the tragedy of love, but love's triumphal hymn.'

The love which shines so gloriously through this period of Shakespeare's work is as mysterious and natural as birth. It is a thing that happens; to ask why it happens is to wait till doomsday for an answer; and if these lovers ask each other, they can only make up jesting replies. When Phebe applies Marlowe's line to her own sudden love of Rosalind-Ganymede, she speaks for them all, men and women alike.

> Dead Shepherd, now I find thy saw of might:
> 'Who ever loved, that loved not at first sight?'

For the most part they know themselves what has

happened; and even where, as with Benedick and Beatrice, we seem to know it before they do, it is only because of their shyness of themselves and each other, which will not suffer their heads to confess the truth of their hearts. The moment that Benedick and Beatrice open fire on one another we know that they are caught. It is only love that makes a man and a woman single out each other for such teasing.

> *Beatrice.* I wonder that you will still be talking, Signior Benedick; nobody marks you.
>
> *Benedick.* What! My dear Lady Disdain, are you yet living?

Benedick might have called her the dear lady of his heart and had done with it, for he gave himself as completely away in that address as he could ever have done in the sonnet they found in his pocket at church, in which no doubt he rhymed, as he feared to rhyme, 'ladies' and 'babies'. Yet, though *Much Ado about Nothing* has precisely the same radiant substance as the rest of the love-comedies—love at first sight—it stands apart from them because the drama itself consists in the delicate working out of the psychology of this heavenly condition. It is not entangled with alien accidents, and owes nothing to the enchantment of disguise; it deals, with an absolute perfection of art, with the process by which the message of unhesitating love steals from the heart to the mind. For this cause it is at once the simplest and the subtlest of all Shakespeare's comedies of love. For once Shakespeare chose to communicate the reality of love to us realistically: we can imagine the essence of the play—for what does Don John matter?— being played in real life at this very moment in the garden of any kindly country house; the process is as old as the hills and as new as the morning.

But generally Shakespeare preferred to let one of his lovers or both know at once what had happened to them. The recognition is as quick as the love of Celia and Oliver.

'Your brother and my sister no sooner met but they looked; no sooner looked but they loved; no sooner loved but they sighed; no sooner sighed but they asked one another the reason; no sooner knew the reason but they sought the remedy.'

The condition is presented to us a thing elemental, inscrutable, which either is or is not. But if it is, Shakespeare can prove to us immediately that it is the true metal. He does not profess to show how it happens; he does something far more difficult; he convinces us that it has happened. He makes his lovers say the simplest and divinest things; they seem to drop sunbeams from their lips. In reality love is too often tongue-tied: Shakespeare gives it speech that seems as natural and magical as love itself. When Orlando says of Rosalind that she is 'just as high as his heart', when Rosalind says that 'men have died from time to time, and worms have eaten them, but not for love', when Beatrice answers the Prince's 'Out of question you were born in a merry hour',

'No, sure, my Lord, my mother cried, but then there was a star danced, and under that I was born,'

we recognize the speech of love as surely as the old prophets recognized the voice of the Lord. This is how lovers would speak if they could. What wonder that they should have recognized their spokesman, and with a single voice elected him the poet laureate of love?

So natural is this flowering that we cannot imagine any end to it but the perfect happiness of marriage.

These lovers are too open-eyed to be victims of the sad illusion; their felicity is destined to outlive beauty's outward. They seem to be poised in a balance of perfect equality; yet if we have to pronounce which way the scale imperceptibly inclines we must say it is to the woman's side. The Duke says to Cesario:

> For, boy, however we do praise ourselves,
> Our fancies are more giddy and unfirm,
> More longing, wavering, sooner lost and worn
> Than women's are.

Certainly the Duke himself changed his affection quickly from Olivia to Viola; but then we may truly urge that he was in love with Cesario all the while. Claudio suspected Hero suddenly and condemned her violently. But these, after all, are only the subordinate necessities of the romantic fable; they do not determine the quality of the belief with which Shakespeare charged it.

The happiness of the love in the mature comedies passes undisturbed into the married security of *Henry IV* and *Julius Caesar*. Kate and Hotspur are the proof that marriage, which is the inevitable end of Shakespeare's lovers, born not merely under a lucky but a dancing star, does not mean the end of love-making.

> I' faith I'll break thy little finger, Harry,
> An if thou wilt not tell me all things true.

They are married, and as much in love as when first they met. There is no room for such gaiety between Brutus and Portia. Brutus is caught in a conspiracy, and is venturing his life in an enterprise which Portia feels must bring disaster. Only the anxiety and devotion can appear, but it is equal. Portia knows that her husband cannot resist her appeal to 'the great vow which did incorporate and make them one'.

> Dwell I but in the suburbs
> Of your good pleasure? If it be no more,
> Portia is Brutus' harlot, not his wife.

And even in the relation of Mistress Quickly and Doll Tearsheet to Falstaff we catch the undertone of a fidelity not altogether unworthy to be compared to this. Both these women loved the genial old ruffian, who in his way loved them; and there are moments when nothing in Shakespeare seems to reveal more clearly his faith in the loyalty of love than the words he makes the cockney landlady say of Falstaff's death:

Nym. They say he cried out of sack.
Host. Ay, that a' did.
Bard. And of women.
Host. Nay, that a' did not.
Boy. Yes, that a' did; and said they were devils incarnate.
Host. A' never could abide carnation; 'twas a colour he never liked.
Boy. A' said once, the devil would have him about women.
Host. A' did in some sort, indeed, handle women; but then he was rheumatic, and talked of the whore of Babylon.

Then comes an abrupt and startling change. Suddenly the steady, shining stream of Shakespeare's presentation of love as happiness and loyalty is disturbed and muddied. The moment coincides with a sudden check in the confident advance of Shakespeare as a poet and a dramatist. We are confronted with what we may roughly call 'the Hamlet period', which includes that strange *sosie* of *Hamlet*, *Measure for Measure*, *Troilus and Cressida*, and *All's Well that Ends Well*. In all these plays there are sustained passages of poetry of form and content incomparable, in which Shakespeare definitely

passes beyond the highest point that poetry had reached
before him, or has reached after him. It was no even
temporary weakening of his purely poetic powers that
assailed him; but we have a sudden sense of loss of all
direction, an invasion of bitterness, of cynicism, and of
a conscious helplessness. We feel we are in contact with
a wounded and bewildered spirit that can see life steadily
and whole no more. Shakespeare managed to project
this bewilderment out of himself most completely and
almost to master it in the realm of art in *Hamlet*. He
concentrated it all in a character, divided in his deepest
being against himself, but yet one; nevertheless the play
is bewildering: not, we believe, because there may be
remnants of an old play in it—Shakespeare had re-
written old plays before without leaving us in any doubt of
his dramatic intention—but simply because the attitude
to life which every great poet must convey had suffered
a chaotic disturbance. We feel the same indecision in
All 's Well. Here also we are told that the unsatisfactory
nature of the whole composed of such brilliant parts is
due to its being a revision of an earlier *Love's Labour
Won*. Again we must reply that Shakespeare knew how
to rewrite plays; he had spent his life at the business.
What we seek to know is the reason why he suddenly
began to fail in a task he had performed for years with
brilliant success, and was to perform again more
marvellously still.

When we find precisely the same fundamental indecision, the same deep hesitation of a mind that can
by nature never be more than half-cynical, in the two
other plays of this period, against which the defect of
rehashing has not yet been urged; when we find that
those four plays are as closely united to each other as
they are separate from the whole of the rest of Shake-

speare's work, we may fairly neglect the hypothetical
'Ur-Hamlets' and earlier versions and stick to what we
have. Of these four plays we may say that we do not
clearly understand Shakespeare's dramatic purpose or
the direction of his sentiment in any of them. Whether
the cause of this clouding actually lay, as we ourselves
sometimes incline to believe, in the love-catastrophe
recorded in the Sonnets, is a minor matter; but the fact
is that the disturbance is most clearly to be distinguished
in his treatment of love. The main intention of *Hamlet*
is on the whole fairly clear. But who has ever spoken
convincingly on the significance of Hamlet's love for
Ophelia? It remains mysterious to us. The final effect
of *Troilus and Cressida* is a feeling that again Shakespeare
could not really face his own subject. For a moment he
handles the love of Troilus and Cressida firmly, then he
appears to let it drop as though it were unbearable and
to turn away to deride the Homeric heroes and the idea
of chivalry. In a play which contains, in Ulysses'
speeches and Troilus' love addresses, some of Shakespeare's finest poetry, we are struck at the last chiefly
by its strange inferiority to Chaucer's wonderful poem.
Shakespeare could have handled the love theme with
the mastery of his great predecessor; but something
prevented him, and the consequence of his hesitation
is that essays are now written to prove that he meant
only a satire on hero-worship. Seeing that Shakespeare
put his finest declaration of the ideal of love into the
play, we may assume that this master of love would
have worked out the tragedy of love if he could have
borne to do so.

Measure for Measure is that one of Shakespeare's plays
which Coleridge could never bring himself to like. The
treatment of love in it is as near to pure cynicism as

Shakespeare could get. Claudio, who really loves, and is loved by Julietta, is sentenced to death for anticipating the marriage he intends. Isabel, who will not sacrifice her chastity to save her brother, ends by acting like a woman of the town, but one utterly devoid of the humanity which glows in Doll Tearsheet or Bianca. Believing her brother dead, she pleads for Angelo, the reverend justice who has killed him and would have ravished her, in these terms:

> Look, if it please you, on this man condemn'd,
> As if my brother lived: I partly think
> A due sincerity govern'd his deeds,
> Till he did look on me; since it is so,
> Let him not die. My brother had but justice,
> In that he did the thing for which he died:
> For Angelo,
> His act did not o'ertake his bad intent,
> And must be buried but as an intent
> That perish'd by the way: thoughts are no subjects;
> Intents but merely thoughts.

This is the reverse of *spretae injuria formae*, with a vengeance. Dr. Johnson's note on it is properly cynical, but it is too good-humoured. The lines contain a fierce and bitter caricature of love, and we must believe that Shakespeare meant it. Then there is the trick, significantly repeated in *All 's Well*, by which Angelo possessed the faithful Mariana in the belief that she was Isabel. And over the whole play hangs the sinister cloud of preoccupation with death, suddenly crystallized into the sardonic figure of Barnardine. Whatever may be the dramatic purpose of this singular 'comedy', the condition of mind from which it sprang is manifest. Life is hateful and contemptible; and as for love, your bawd is your only honest man.

In *All's Well that Ends Well*—supremely cynical title—Shakespeare seems deliberately to take revenge on his own idealism of love. He deliberately makes Bertram detestable and shows that the bragging coward, Parolles, is the better man. Then he makes Helena fall in love, passionately, tenderly, delicately, with the unpleasant young nobleman, builds her up as surely as Beatrice or Rosalind, puts into her mouth the divinely hesitating reply to Bertram's purely brutal 'What would you have?'

> Something; and scarce so much: nothing, indeed.
> I would not tell you what I would, my lord:—
> Faith, yes;
> Strangers and foes do sunder and not kiss.

Yet after all this she plays the Mariana trick. One wonders what can be the conception of the poet in the minds of those who imagine that he had written a romantic comedy with a happy ending. The self-torturing mood of the play, the bitter mood of 'I'll show you a happy ending', is only too apparent. But Shakespeare, it seems, could never succeed in projecting an attitude of embitterment completely: his hand weakened, his idealization of love and humanity interfered. That is one reason why the fascination of the plays of this strange period is out of all proportion to the sureness of their achievement as works of dramatic art.

We may speculate that the true poetic realization of this period, whose stress we imagine we can measure by Othello's words—'when I love thee not Chaos is come again'—is to be found in the great tragedies. The shattering personal experience there found its place in a vision of life as a whole. There is no bitterness any more; and in the microcosm of his vision of life which is his attitude to love it is apparent that Shakespeare

has regained his belief. The love of Othello and Desdemona is in itself unclouded. No human mind could
resist the villainy of Iago. Their perfect happiness is
overwhelmed by no defect of their love, and Othello's
very act of murder is, as Coleridge said, an act of
sacrifice to love; it is the tragedy of an ideal shattered
by an alien power. Had there been no Iago their love
would have endured to death. So, too, with the miniature of this great picture of married happiness, which
we have in *Coriolanus*. Virgilia's reticent devotion to her
proud and passionate husband is matched by his gentle-
ness in her presence. Her 'gracious silence' wields a
charm over him which Shakespeare makes us feel completely in the few dozen lines he gives to her. In *Macbeth*
also, though the bond holds between natures far darker
than these, it holds unbreakable. Lady Macbeth may
be her husband's evil genius, but she is united to him
more deeply by their love than their crime. And of
Antony and Cleopatra, with even more force than of *Romeo
and Juliet*, it may be said that it is a triumph rather than
a tragedy of love. At the last the mutual devotion is
complete. Cleopatra in her death-scene remains what
she has been, capricious as she is passionate; but her
surrender is entire. 'Husband, I come. Now to that
name my courage prove my title.' It is a love which
may not promise the golden happiness on which Shakespeare so fondly dwelt, but it is one which transfigures
the lovers and lifts them to heights of feeling and sacrifice of which neither they nor we had dreamed.

Shakespeare's final period is one of return to the love
of his youth. During the great tragedies love had been
on the whole—save in *Antony and Cleopatra*—a subordinate issue. He had other things to convey—the conclusion of his brooding on his experience of that life of

which love is a mighty part, but only a part. Yet we may discover how great a part it was to him by his return to the theme in all his three last plays, *The Winter's Tale*, *Cymbeline*, and *The Tempest*. We feel that it was only the love scenes of the first two of these that deeply interested him. In those scenes his touch is perfectly firm, his mastery evident, while in the rest it is hesitating and perfunctory. But something ethereal is added to the love of the earlier comedies and something earthly taken away. The light is no longer golden but silver. Lovers are no more witty together; they are almost enfolded in a dream of tenderness. After the wild storm of the tragedies, culminating in *King Lear*, we hear the poet proclaiming through Florizel and Perdita, Imogen and Posthumus, Ferdinand and Miranda, that love is the only light to follow. The message sounds with a magical clearness in the silver note of *The Tempest*. The wise magician throws away his book: he has seen his vision of human life.

> The cloud-capp'd towers, the gorgeous palaces,
> The solemn temples, the great globe itself,
> Yea, all which it inherit, shall dissolve
> And, like this insubstantial pageant faded,
> Leave not a wrack behind. We are such stuff
> As dreams are made on, and our little life
> Is rounded with a sleep.

Yet with his wisdom and his pain of heart, Prospero gives way to the faith and the freedom of love; and his creator looks at the world not through his eyes only, but through Miranda's also.

> O, wonder!
> How many goodly creatures are there here!
> How beauteous mankind is! O brave new world,
> That has such people in't!

So 'the world's great age begins anew'. The magic of Shakespeare's last enchantment is that he makes us for a moment believe that the eyes of love alone can see the miracle; and perhaps it is the ultimate truth of life that indeed they do.

[SEPTEMBER 1921.

A NEGLECTED HEROINE OF SHAKESPEARE

CORIOLANUS is, if not one of the greatest, one of the most masterly of Shakespeare's plays. If it does not hold all the spiritual significance of any of the three great tragedies, if it has not the profound emotional appeal of *Antony and Cleopatra* or *Julius Caesar*, it indubitably belongs to the same period of serene mastery of theme and expression. French critics continually, and English critics occasionally—these last unnecessarily humble before the prestige of French criticism—have said that *Coriolanus* is Shakespeare's most perfect work of art. While we deplore their language, we understand their meaning. *Coriolanus* is a magnificent example of creative control. Its design is, as Mr. Walter Sickert has well said of Poussin's painting, 'marshalled'. Its economy, its swiftness, its solidity, its astonishing clarity and pregnancy of language are not only satisfying and exhilarating in themselves, but may have a peculiar and profound appropriateness to the warlike argument. Just as the looser texture of *Antony and Cleopatra* seems to be the inevitable garment of the decaying soldiership of Antony, so the exact and unrelenting pattern of *Coriolanus* seems essential to the unfaltering decision and the unswerving success of the earlier Roman general. The play marches onward like a legion in the days when Roman soldiers were Romans still.

Perhaps it is this quality of Roman relentlessness and inevitability which has made it unsympathetic to the general English taste, for among us it is surely the least popular of Shakespeare's great plays. In France, on the contrary, it is said to be the most popular; probably not for the same reason. Beyond the fact that Coriolanus is a familiar and traditional hero of the French theatre, the concentrated and controlled dramatic action which distinguishes Shakespeare's *Coriolanus* from his other great dramas appeals directly to the French taste. Since, however, this only means that *Coriolanus* is an unusually well-constructed play, it cannot account for the general reluctance of English people to admit it to their affections. The reason, one imagines, is that it is too Roman. An English audience, and English readers, for that matter, like to surrender themselves to their heroes. They can idolize Brutus as an eloquent Hampden, and sympathize with an Antony lost in the embraces of his serpent of old Nile. A martyr for political liberty, a martyr for love, these are intimate and comprehensible to us; but a martyr to the aristocratic idea is not. He is an alien; we have too much of the British constitution in ourselves for him to warm our blood.

In other words, Coriolanus is an unsympathetic hero, and all the characters of the play, save one, to whom we shall return, strike chill upon the general heart. Volumnia is altogether too much like that forbidding Spartan mother who haunted our schooldays with her grim farewell, 'Return with your shield or upon it'; Menenius is too cynical, too worldly-wise to move us humanly in his discomfiture; Brutus and Sicinius arouse neither sympathy nor disdain; and the emotion we feel at the knightly generosity of Aufidius is dashed too soon by his confession that, if he cannot overthrow Coriolanus by fair means, he will by foul. Coriolanus himself we cannot like, any more than a schoolboy can like Themistocles. One may despise one's country, one may hate one's country, but one may not lead an enemy against her. These are primitive ethics, no doubt, but they are profound, and though they may be alien to aesthetic criticism, they have their roots deep in the human heart. The writer who ignores them deliberately imperils the universality of his appeal.

We can see clearly enough why *Coriolanus* should be that among Shakespeare's greater plays which is most neglected by the public, and therefore the least familiar to the stage. It is not so easy to understand why it should have been so neglected by the critics, unless perhaps they are not quite so immune from the effects of instinctive sympathy as in theory they ought to be. By the critics I mean the true literary critics, not the textual 'philologers'. These have been busy enough, sometimes to good effect, as with the whole line which they have neatly restored from North's Plutarch, but at least as often in a spirit perhaps best described as one of slight impatience with poetry. This is, however, not the occasion to catalogue the things they have done which they ought not to have done; but only to try to show that they have also left undone a few things that they ought to have done. Far from me at this moment the desire to shiver a lance in open battle with the editors; I only crave their leave to ride to the rescue of an all but vanished lady to whom they have had no time to stretch out a helping hand.

All that needs to be premised is the simple fact that *Coriolanus* was first printed in the Folio of 1623, and that we have no other authority for the text. On the whole we may say that the Folio text is careless enough, although I believe that—obvious misprints apart—it is at least as near to Shakespeare's original as most modern recensions, which take us as much farther away by some of their readings as they bring us nearer to it by others. The most persistent weakness of the Folio *Coriolanus* is the haphazard distribution of lines among the speakers. One of the most palpable of these blunders has been rectified by common consent. In Act III (Sc. i, l. 237) when Menenius is trying hard to persuade Coriolanus to moderate his contemptuous language towards the plebs, the Folio gives him these impossible words:

> I would they were barbarians, as they are,
> Though in Rome litter'd: not Romans, as they are not,
> Though calved i' th' porch o' th' Capitol:

It is as certain that Menenius did not speak them as it is certain that Coriolanus did. They have been properly restored to the hero. The Folio *Coriolanus* then, although the true and authentic original, is far from impeccable.

So much by way of preamble to the attempt at rescue.

Of all the characters in *Coriolanus* one alone can be said to be truly congenial; and she is the least substantial of them all. Virgilia, Coriolanus' wife, though she is present throughout the whole of four scenes, speaks barely a hundred words. But a sudden, direct light is cast upon her by a phrase which takes our breaths with beauty, when Coriolanus welcomes her on his triumphant return from Corioli as 'My gracious silence!' Magical words! They give a miraculous substance to our fleeting, fading glimpses of a lovely vision which seems to tremble away from the clash of arms and pride that reverberates through the play. Behind the haughty warrior and his Amazonian mother, behind the vehement speech of this double Lucifer, the exquisite, timid spirit of Virgilia shrinks out of sight into the haven of her quiet home. One can almost hear the faint click of the door behind her as it shuts her from the noise of brawling tongues. Yet in her presence, and in the memory of her presence, Coriolanus becomes

another and a different being. It is true we may listen
in vain for other words so tender as 'My gracious silence!'
from his lips. A man who has one love alone finds only
one such phrase in a lifetime. But in the heat of victorious battle, when Coriolanus would clasp Cominius
in his arms for joy, he discovers in himself another splendid phrase to remember his happiness with Virgilia.

>   Oh! let me clip ye
> In arms as sound as when I woo'd, in heart
> As merry, as when our nuptial day was done
> And tapers burned to bedward.

And even in the anguish of the final struggle between
his honour and his heart, when his wife comes with his
mother to intercede for Rome, it is in the very accents
of passionate devotion that he cries to Virgilia,

>   Best of my flesh!
> Forgive my tyranny; but do not say,
> 'For that forgive our Romans.' Oh! a kiss
> Long as my exile, sweet as my revenge!
> Now, by the jealous queen of heaven, that kiss
> I carried from thee, dear, and my true lip
> Hath virgin'd it e'er since.

In the proud, unrelenting man of arms these sudden
softenings are wonderful. They conjure up the picture
of a more reticent and self-suppressed Othello, and we
feel that, to strike to the heart through Coriolanus'
coat of mail, it needed an unfamiliar beauty of soul,
a woman whose delicate nature stood apart, untouched
by the broils and furies of her lord's incessant battling
with the Roman people and the enemies of Rome.

In the play Virgilia speaks barely a hundred words.
But they are truly the speech of a 'gracious silence', as
precious and revealing as they are rare. She appears
first (Act I, Sc. 3) in her own house, sitting silent

at her sewing. Coriolanus has gone to the wars. Volumnia tries to kindle her with something of her own Amazonian ecstasy at the thought of men in battle. 'I tell thee, daughter, I sprang not more in joy at first hearing he was a man child than now in first seeing he had proved himself a man.' Virgilia's reply, the first words she speaks in the play, touch to the quick of the reality of war and her own unquiet mind.

> But had he died in the business, madam; how then?

The thoughts of her silence thus revealed, she says no more until chattering Valeria, for all the world like one of the fashionable ladies in Colonel Repington's diary, is announced. She has come to drag her out to pay calls. Virgilia tries to withdraw. Volumnia will not let her, and even while the maid is in the room waiting to know whether she may show Valeria in, she bursts into another ecstatic vision of her son in the midst of battle, 'his bloody brow with his mailed hand then wiping'. Again Virgilia reveals herself.

> His bloody brow? O Jupiter, no blood!

Valeria enters on a wave of small talk. She has seen Virgilia's little boy playing. The very image of his father; 'has such a confirmed countenance'. She had watched him chase a butterfly, catching it and letting it go, again and again. 'He did so set his teeth and tear it. Oh, I warrant how he mammocked it!'

Volum. One on 's father's moods.
Val. Indeed, la, 'tis a noble child.
Virg. A crack, madam.

'An *imp*, madam!' The meaning leaps out of the half-contemptuous word. Don't call him a noble child for his childish brutality. It pains, not rejoices Virgilia.

Nor, for all the persuasions of Volumnia and Valeria, will she stir out of the house. She does not want society; she cannot visit 'the good lady that lies in'. She is as firm as she is gentle.

'Tis not to save labour, nor that I want love.

Simply that she is anxious and preoccupied. She will not 'turn her solemness out o' door'; she cannot. Coriolanus is at the wars.

So, in two dozen words and a world of unspoken contrast Virgilia is given to us: her horror of brutality and bloodshed, her anxiety for her husband, her reticence, her firmness. She is not a bundle of nerves, but she is full of the aching fears of love. Truly, 'a gracious silence'.

She next appears when the news is come that Coriolanus has triumphed (Act II, Sc. 1). Volumnia and Valeria are talking with Menenius. She stands aside listening. He is sure to be wounded, says Menenius; he always is. She breaks out: 'Oh, no, no, no!' She retires into her silence again while Volumnia and Menenius talk proudly on. 'In troth, there's wondrous things spoken of him,' says chattering Valeria. Virgilia murmurs: 'The gods grant them true!' 'True! Pow, wow!' says Volumnia, in hateful scorn: one can see her sudden turn, hear her rasping voice. Virgilia is not one of the true breed of Roman wives and mothers. And indeed she is not. She is thinking of wounds, not as glorious marks of bravery, but as the mutilated body of the man she adores. Wounds, wounds! They talk of nothing but wounds. Virgilia suffers in silence. Coriolanus is wounded. That is a world wounded to her.

Coriolanus enters, crowned with the oaken garland and swathed in bandages, unrecognizable. He kneels before his mother. Then he sees Virgilia, standing apart, weeping silently. These are the words of the Folio text. Only the spelling has been modernized; the punctuation has been left untouched.

> *Corio.* My gracious silence, hail:
>   Would'st thou have laugh'd, had I come coffin'd home,
>   That weep'st to see me triumph? Ah my dear,
>   Such eyes the widows in Corioli wear
>   And mothers that lack sons.
> *Mene.* Now the Gods crown thee.
> *Com.* And live you yet? Oh my sweet Lady, pardon.
> *Volum.* I know not where to turn.
>   Oh welcome home: and welcome General,
>   And y'are welcome all.

The first two of these speeches and their speakers contain no difficulty. But, obviously, 'And live you yet? Oh, my sweet Lady, pardon,' does not belong to Cominius. On his lips it is nonsense. The editors have resolved the problem by giving the line to Coriolanus, and the following speech of Volumnia to Valeria. Corilanus is supposed to say to Menenius, 'And live you yet!' then, suddenly catching sight of Valeria, to beg her pardon for not having seen her before.

We have a free hand in disposing of the line. There is no objection to Volumnia's speech being given to Valeria, whose effusive manner it suits better. But to make Coriolanus surprised that Menenius is still alive is pointless; he had no reason to suppose that the arm-chair hero was dead. Moreover, to make him turn to Valeria, and say, 'Oh, my sweet Lady, pardon,' is to give the great warrior the manners of a carpet knight.

Now think of the relation between Virgilia and Coriolanus; remember how her imagination has been preoccupied by his wounds; see her in imagination weeping at the pitiful sight of her wounded husband—

and read the lines through without regard to the speakers. It will, I believe, occur to any one with an instinct for psychology that 'And live you yet?' may take up Coriolanus' previous words. 'Ah, my dear,' he has said, 'it is the women who have no husbands who weep as you do.' Then, and not till then, Virgilia breaks silence. 'And live you yet!' And are you really my husband? Is this thing of bandages the lord of my heart? At her sudden, passionate words, Coriolanus understands her tears. He has a glimpse of the anguish of her love. He has been an unimaginative fool. 'Oh, my sweet Lady, pardon!' This, I suggest, is the way the passage should be read:

> *Corio.*   Ah my dear,
>   Such eyes the widows in Corioli wear
>   And mothers that lack sons.
> *Mene.* Now the gods crown thee!
> *Virg.* And live you yet?
> *Corio.* Oh, my sweet lady, pardon . . .
> *Val.* I know not where to turn.

And to my own mind it is an essential part of the beauty of the passage that these few lightning words of love should flash through the hubbub of Menenius' welcome and Valeria's effusive congratulations.[1]

Virgilia appears again in the scene following Coriolanus' banishment (Act IV, Sc. 2). Here the alterations necessary are self-evident, and it is difficult to understand why they have not been made before. Again the test of reading through the short scene with an imaginative realization of Virgilia must be applied. Again her exquisite timidity of speech must be contrasted, as Shakespeare deliberately contrasted it, with Volumnia's

---

[1] See note, p. 190.

headstrong and contemptuous anger. It will then, I believe, be plain that of Volumnia's final words,

> Anger's my meat; I sup upon my self
> And so shall starve with feeding. Come, let's go.
> Leave this faint puling and lament as I do,
> In anger, Juno-like. Come, come, come,

the last two lines are addressed to Virgilia alone. Besides Volumnia herself only Menenius is there. The lines cannot be spoken to him. Only Virgilia remains. She is not angry, but sad, at Coriolanus' banishment, just as in his triumph she was sad, not joyful: and just as then, Volumnia scorns her for her weakness.

Now read again the Folio text, which is that of the modern editions, of lines 11–28. Volumnia meets the two tribunes who have been the prime movers in her son's banishment:

Volum. Oh y'are well met:
    Th' hoarded plague a' th' gods requite your love. (10)
Mene. Peace, peace, be not so loud.
Volum. If that I could for weeping, you should hear,
    Nay, and you shall heare some. Will you be gone?
Virg. You shall stay too: I would I had the power
    To say so to my husband. (15)
Sicin. Are you mankind?
Volum. Aye, fool, is that a shame. Note but this, fool,
    Was not a man my father? Had'st thou foxship
    To banish him that struck more blows for Rome
    Than thou hast spoken words.
Sicin. Oh blessed Heavens! (20)
Volum. More noble blows than ever thou wise words.
    And for Rome's good, I'll tell thee what: yet go:
    Nay, but thou shalt stay too: I would my son
    Were in Arabia, and thy tribe before him,
    His good sword in his hand. (25)

Sicin. What then?
Virg. What then? He'ld make an end of thy posterity
Volum. Bastards, and all.
    Good man, the wounds that he does bear for Rome!

It is obvious that the peremptory 'You shall stay too!'
(l. 14) is not spoken by Virgilia. It is as completely
discordant with her character, and with Volumnia's
description of her behaviour during the scene ('this
faint puling') as it is accordant with the character of
Volumnia. Volumnia forces first one, then the other
tribune to stay; we can see her clutch them by the
sleeve, one in either of her nervous hands. At her words
Virgilia interposes a sighing aside, 'Would I had the
power to say so to my husband!'

It is equally clear that Virgilia cannot possibly have
indulged in the imagination of line 27. 'What then?
He'd make an end of thy posterity.' There is no stop at
the end of the line in the Folio; it runs on to the next
half line; and the whole line and a half undoubtedly
belong to Volumnia. A simple transposition of the
rubrics is all that is needed.

Volum.   What then?
    He'ld make an end of thy posterity,
    Bastards and all.
Virg. Good man, the wounds that he does bear for Rome!

It is another sighing aside and another indication that
Virgilia is haunted by the memory of those wounds she
could not bear to see. Unless these asides are restored
to her, and the brutal words taken away, quite apart
from the violation of her character, Volumnia's final
sneer at her 'faint puling' is ridiculous.

Virgilia appears for the last time as the silent partici-
pant in Volumnia's embassy of intercession. For the

first and only time a bodily vision of her beauty is given
to us, when Coriolanus cries:

> What is that curt'sy worth? Or those dove's eyes
> Which can make gods forsworn? I melt, and am not
> Of stronger earth than others.

She has no need of words to make her appeal; her eyes
speak for her. She says simply:

> My lord and husband!

Corio. These eyes are not the same I wore in Rome.
Virg. The sorrow that delivers us thus changed
  Makes you think so.
Corio.   Like a dull actor now,
  I have forgot my part, and I am out,
  Even to a full disgrace. Best of my flesh,
  Forgive my tyranny: but do not say,
  'For that forgive our Romans.' Oh! a kiss
  Long as my exile, sweet as my revenge!
  Now, by the jealous queen of heaven, that kiss
  I carried from thee, dear; and my true lip
  Hath virgin'd it e'er since.

After this Virgilia speaks but a single sentence more.
Volumnia ends her pleading with an impassioned ad-
juration to her son:

> For myself, son,
> I purpose not to wait on Fortune, till
> These wars determine: if I cannot persuade thee
> Rather to show a noble grace to both parts
> Than seek the end of one, thou shalt no sooner
> March to assault thy country, than to tread—
> Trust to't, thou shalt not—on thy mother's womb
> That brought thee to this world.

Virg.   Ay, and mine
  That brought you forth this boy, to keep your name
  Living to time.

Virgilia's words contain much in little space. They,

her last words in the play, are the first in which she shows herself at one with her husband's mother. Always before, Volumnia has been angry, impatient, and contemptuous towards Virgilia; and Virgilia had held her peace without yielding an inch of ground to Volumnia's vehemence. We have felt throughout that they are the embodiments of two opposed spirits—of pride and love. Not that Volumnia's pride has now changed to love; it is the same pride of race that moves her, the fear of disgrace to a noble name:

> The end of war 's uncertain; but this is certain,
> That, if thou conquer Rome, the benefit
> Which thou shalt thereby reap is such a name
> Whose repetition will be dogged with curses,
> Whose chronicle thus writ: 'The man was noble
> But with his last attempt he wip'd it out,
> Destroy'd his country, and his name remains
> To the ensuing age abhorr'd.'

But now these spirits of love and pride are reconciled; for once they make the same demand. Volumnia pleads that her son shall remember honour, Virgilia that her husband shall remember mercy. The double appeal is too strong. Coriolanus yields to it, and pays the penalty.

Not one of the readjustments suggested in this essay calls for the alteration of a single word in the text of the Folio. They consist solely in a redistribution of words among the speakers, and in the most complicated instance a redistribution of some kind has long since been seen to be necessary and long since been made. I venture to think that together they will help to disengage the true outline of one of Shakespeare's most delicate minor heroines. There was no place for a Desdemona in the story of Coriolanus; but in a few firm touches Shakespeare has given us a woman whose silence

we can feel to be the unspoken judgement on the pride
of arms and the pride of race which are the theme of
the play.

For it is surely not against the democratic idea that
Coriolanus is tried and found wanting. In spite of
Signor Croce's assurance to the contrary, it is impossible
to believe that the contempt for the city mob with which
the play is penetrated was not shared by Shakespeare
himself. The greatest writers strive to be impersonal,
and on the whole they achieve impersonality; but,
though they carve out an image that is not wholly like
themselves, they cannot work wholly against the grain
of their own convictions. Prejudice will out. And the
aversion from the city mob which is continually expressed in Shakespeare's work and comes to a head in
Coriolanus was indubitably his own. It is indeed less
plausible to deny this than it would be to argue that at
a time when his genius was seizing on themes of a
greater tragic scope it was his sympathy with the anti-
plebeian colour of the Coriolanus story that led Shakespeare to choose it for his play.

This is not a question of Shakespeare's political views.
We do not know what they were, and we do no more
than guess at them. Signor Croce is thus far right.
But when he goes on to assure us that it is a wild goose
chase to look to discover where Shakespeare's sympathies lay in the world in which he lived, we can point
to the knowledge we actually have of every great
writer. We do know their sympathies. It may be an
illegitimate knowledge, but the laws it violates are laws
of Signor Croce's own devising. It is his own logical fiat
that holds the kingdoms of the aesthetic and the practical
asunder. In fact, there is no dividing line between
them. A writer's predispositions in practical life do

constantly colour his aesthetic creation, and every great writer who has been conscious of his activity has either confessed the fact or gloried in it.

We know that Shakespeare disliked the city mob. If we care to know why we have only to exercise a little imagination and picture to ourselves the finest creative spirit in the world acting in his own plays before a pitful of uncomprehending, base mechanicals.

> Alas, 'tis true, I have gone here and there
> And made myself a motley to the view,
> Gored mine own thoughts, sold cheap what is most dear.

The man who used that terrible phrase, who 'gored his own thoughts' to wring shillings from the pockets of the greasy, grinning crowd in front of him, had no cause to love them; and Shakespeare did not. He was an aristocrat, not in the political sense, but as every man of fine nerves who shrinks from contact with the coarse-nerved is an aristocrat, as Anton Tchehov was an aristocrat when he wrote, 'Alas, I shall never be a Tolstoyan. In women I love beauty above all things, and in the history of mankind, culture expressed in carpets, spring carriages, and keenness of wit.'

Shakespeare could not therefore measure Coriolanus against the democratic idea in which he did not believe; nor could he pit the patriotic idea against him, for Coriolanus was immune from a weakness for his country. It is domestic love that pierces his armour and inflicts the mortal wound. And perhaps in Shakespeare's mind the power of that love was manifested less in the speech of the vehement and eloquent Volumnia than in the silence of the more delicate woman to whom we have attempted to restore a few of her precious words.

[SEPTEMBER 1921.

III

BURTON'S 'ANATOMY'

ABOUT three hundred years ago was published in Oxford, where it had been composed, 'The Anatomy of Melancholy, what it is, with all the kinds, causes, symptoms, prognostics, and several cures of it. In three partitions; with their several sections, members, and subsections, philosophically, medicinally, historically opened and cut up by Democritus Junior.' Within fifty years the original quarto had grown into a folio, passed through eight editions, and—so the story runs—enriched its publisher with an estate. That Robert Burton, the author, student of Christ Church and vicar of St. Thomas, Oxford, derived any profit from a book which was the encyclopaedia of the men of letters and the diversion of the dilettanti throughout the seventeenth century, there is no evidence and little probability. One can hardly imagine 'the melancholy man' making a profit out of anything.

With the changed taste of the eighteenth century the *Anatomy* lost its popularity and became the precious possession of the few. Warton imagined that he had discovered in it the source of Milton's *Allegro* and *Penseroso*, and he may have been right. Dr. Johnson told Boswell—perhaps with a touch of rhetorical exaggeration—that it was 'the only book that ever took him out of bed two hours earlier than he wished to rise'; Laurence Sterne indubitably made good and copious use of it to embellish *Tristram Shandy*; and at the turn of the century—ten editions carried Burton down to 1800—Charles Lamb was completely convinced that he was caviare to the general. 'I do not know', he wrote

D

of the two-volume edition published in 1813, 'a more heartless sight than the reprint of the *A. of M.* What need was there of unearthing the bones of that fantastic great old man, to expose them in a winding-sheet of the newest fashion to modern censure? What hapless stationer could dream of Burton ever becoming popular?' Lamb should not have lamented; that new edition gained for Burton one of his aptest readers—Keats, who borrowed from it (and properly acknowledged his debt) the story of Lamia, and some of the bitterest eloquence in his *Ode to Fanny*. Still, though Keats made splendid use of the *Anatomy*, we may admit that Lamb had a privilege of possession; he was Burton's ideal reader, and he was almost entitled to supply from his own imagination, as in fact he tried to do, some posthumous fragments from the commonplace book which Burton did not leave behind him.

The one he did leave behind is the *Anatomy*. For what is that indescribable volume but the true original Patriarch, the undisputed Sovereign, of all commonplace books whatsoever? It professes to deal with melancholy, but what of that? Melancholy is the merest skeleton of a vast body, no more than the *principium divisionis* of the old logicians; re-shuffle the matter a little, and it would clothe another skeleton just as neatly. It might have been the *Anatomy of the Human Soul*, except that Burton would have found the title too ambitious; to-day it would appear, if it could appear at all, as *Curiosities of Psychology*. *Quidquid agunt homines*—Burton could truly have said—*nostri farrago libelli est*. But it is the world of human action at one remove, a vast repository of what other men had said and thought about it, a museum of the old style, like the Ashmolean of Burton's century, with statues and monsters in spirits and astrolabes and dried crocodiles, and a puckered old curator explaining, describing, moving among the medley, inscrutable, indefatigable, apparently absorbed. The ghost of a half-smile warns us that he may not be altogether serious, but we can never be sure; and even when he suddenly throws the gown of office aside to pour out the vials of his personal indignation, or to tell us some fantastic tale, he gives us no time to parley. Before our astonishment has passed he has slipped into his fortress of folios, against which we may batter at first in vain.

Assuredly Burton does not believe all he tells us; certainly he believes a great deal. But how much, who can say? His capacity for faith in things outside his experience is large and accommodating. We do not need the evidence of the horoscope which he had carved on his tomb, or the legend which tells that he made away with himself in order to die on his prognosticated day, to know that he took astrology seriously; although in his book he professes to have an open mind concerning the influence of the planets upon human destiny, the undertone of belief is audible. But he is prepared to see astrology pass into astronomy; the Copernican revolution is quite acceptable to him; it sorts not only with his skill in mathematics, but with his temperament. 'If it be so that the Earth is a Moon, then are we also giddy, vertiginous, and lunatic within this sublunary maze.' He believes in the sovereign virtue of precious stones, or at least we may deduce belief from the fact that he quotes all the authorities on the one side and none on the other. He stands at the dividing line between the age of superstition and the age of science; for the nature of evidence (as it is called by the moderns) he cares nothing. Everything is admissible that has been written in a book; and the more odd it is, the better for his purposes, provided it has acquired the sanctity of print.

'Being in the country in vacation time not many years since at Lindley, in Leicestershire, my father's house, I first observed this amulet of a spider in a nutshell lapped in silk, so applied for an ague by my mother; whom, although I knew to have excellent skill in chirurgery, sore eyes, aches, etc., and such experimental medicines, as all the country where she dwelt can witness, to have done many famous and good cures upon diverse poor folks, that were otherwise destitute of help: yet among all other experiments, this methought was most absurd and ridiculous. I could see no warrant for it. *Quid aranea cum febre?* For what antipathy? till at length rambling among authors (as I often do) I found this very medicine in Dioscorides, approved by Matthiolus, repeated by Alderovandus *cap. de Aranea, lib. de insectis*, I began to have a better opinion of it.'

Even here we cannot be certain that there is no twinkle in his eye, and that the tale is not being told against himself. But since his face is serious while he tells us of a hundred other remedies as odd, we suspend judgement and are content to be grateful for the one little glimpse of his mother, wife of his 'excellent father', Ralph Burton, Esquire, of Lindley, in Leicestershire, where Robert Burton was born on February 8, 1576.

The little we learn of Burton's life from sources outside his book is useless knowledge. Apart from a meagre handful of dates and the tradition that he used to go down to the waterside at Oxford when his depression was at its blackest and listen to the bargees swearing at one another, 'at which he would set his hands to his sides and laugh profusely', the chroniclers tell us nothing that we cannot discover better from his own pages. Thence we learn the all-important fact that he had a miserable time at the grammar school (at Sutton Coldfield), where he was '*fractus animis*, and moped many times weary of his life'. Probably his schoolboy misery was a prime cause of the depression that dogged him for the rest of his life, though he himself apparently preferred to ascribe it to his 'having Mercury misaffected in his geniture'. Yet it is characteristic of him that, in spite of his hateful memories of his boyhood, he had the kindest recollection of the 'excellent air' of Sutton Coldfield. It is indeed doubly characteristic of him; it shows his instinctive desire to remember the best about everything, and also the pathetic pride he took in any local attachments outside Oxford. He had so few, and he made so much of them. In his chapter on the benefits of good air the poverty of the list of places which he knows is remarkable; but he manages to single out for especial commendation of their salubrity where he went to school, where he was parson, and finally where he was born. Thus he praises—

'places best to me known, upon the river of Anker in Warwickshire, Swarston, and Drakesby-upon-Trent. . . . Sutton Coldfield in Warwickshire (where I was once a grammar scholar) . . . in an excellent air and full of all manner of pleasures . . . Segrave in Leicestershire (wh. town I am now bound to remember) is situated in a champaign at the edge of the wolds, yet no place likely yields a better air.'

He goes on to recommend high places; he mentions only three, and one of these, 'which I may not omit for vicinity's sake,' is 'Oldbury in the confines of Warwickshire, where I have often looked about me with great delight, at the foot of which hill I was born'.

A commoner of Brasenose, a student of Christ Church, an inmate of the Bodleian, Burton seems to have no existence outside Oxford from the end of his schooldays

to his death; we think of him first and foremost as the
affable, familiar ghost of the old University, flitting
from cloister to quadrangle, bewildered and lost if he
stirred abroad. If we look more closely, however, we
can discern in him a hankering after another life, a tinge
of regret for some simpler and less theoretic existence.
Though the traces are slight—what writer has more
sedulously concealed himself than Burton?—they are
conclusive. He never uses the language of affection
when he speaks of Oxford; and when he speaks of the
University with admiration, as he sometimes does, it is
only to greet some startling innovation—the building of
the new waterworks, the foundation of the botanical
garden, or the establishment of the Bishop in a new
palace at Cuddesdon. Had he lived to-day he would
assuredly have urged the case for an electric tramway
down the High. The beauty of the Oxford countryside
is of the rarest, the air of Boars Hill of the finest; he
never mentions them. It is of his other homes alone that
he writes with love and approbation; and we feel that
even his fishing, the only sport he describes with the
glow of actual experience and personal delight, was
done, not on Cherwell or Isis, but somewhere on that
'river of Anker in Warwickshire'.

'Plutarch in his book *De Soler. Animal.* speaks against all
fishing, "as a filthy, base, illiberal employment, having
neither wit nor perspicacity in it, nor worth the labour".
But he that shall consider the variety of baits for all seasons,
and pretty devices which our anglers have invented, peculiar
lines, false flies, several sleights, will say, that it deserves
like commendation, requires as much study and perspicacity
as the rest, and is to be preferred before them. Because
hawking and hunting are very laborious, much riding and
many dangers accompany them: but this is still and quiet:

and if so be the angler catch no fish, yet he hath a wholesome walk to the brookside, pleasant shade by the sweet silver streams: he hath good air, and sweet smells of fine, fresh meadow flowers, he hears the melodious harmony of birds, he sees the swans, herons, ducks, water-horns, coots, and many other fowl, with their brood, which he thinketh better than the noise of hounds, or blast of horns, and all the sport they can make.'

Our sense that Burton felt himself an exile in Oxford and cherished some instinctive resentment against the monastic life of the University accords with the impression made by the most persistent of the personal tones which sound through the *Anatomy*—the bitter complaint of the disappointed scholar. Oxford is a microcosm of the greater world without; advancement goes not by merit, but by favour. He drops into two full pages of Latin to give vent to his indignation. Any academic honour can be bought for money, and the only thought of the officers of the University is that 'those who commence, whether they are taught or untaught is of no moment, shall be sleek, fat pigeons worth the plucking'. Whether Oxford was indeed as corrupt as Burton describes it we do not know, but it is obvious that he found the atmosphere intolerable. Yet what could he do? If he left Oxford, what had the true university scholar, without money or influence, to expect? He may 'teach in a grammar school at a falconer's wages, ten pounds a year', or be trencher chaplain in a gentleman's house, for which service 'he may perchance have a living to halves, or some small rectory with the mother of the maids at length, a poor kinswoman or a cracked chambermaid, to have and to hold during the time of his life.' So he looks back with longing eyes to the days before the Reformation, and regrets the wholesale dis-

ruption of the religious houses by the too 'zealous innova-
tors'. Had they taken thought for the commonweal
instead of their own fortunes they would have preserved
at least one in each part of the country, where true
scholars might have congregated to pursue their studies
in comfort and security and to be a light to the world
about them. Instead of this happy condition the men
of learning are herded together, their talents rusted, and
their lives unprofitably worn away.

'We that are University men, like so many hide-bound
calves in a pasture, tarry out our time, wither away as a
flower ungathered in a garden, and are never used; or as
so many candles, illuminate ourselves alone, obscuring one
another's light, and are not discerned here at all, the least
of which translated to a dark room or some country benefice,
where it might shine apart, would give a fair light and be
seen over all. Whilst we lie waiting here as those sick men
did at the Pool of Bethesda, till the Angel stirred the water,
expecting a good hour, they step between and beguile us of
our preferment.'

Those who know Burton know that this is no merely
personal grievance on which he dwells; and those who
do not may discern in his regret for the wasted Reformation the outlines of an ideal system of provincial
universities which three centuries have not even yet
made a full reality. It is customary to conceive him
only as a bookworm, winding his way through forgotten
authors. He was much more than this. There was a
fine, magnanimous spirit in him which chafed at the
waste not only of his own life, but of all that humanity
and education might accomplish in the world; with this
spirit his great volume was impregnated against the
decay of time, so that even now, if we will only take the
pains to blow the dust off the covers, we shall find

within a freshness, a savour, and sanity for which we were scarce prepared. For the *Anatomy* is a deceptive book; it is a museum which we enter in a mood of idle curiosity and leave thinking less about the multitude of strange things collected there than of the man who gathered them together. At first we catch hardly more from the pages of his book than the hint of a strange, faint fragrance, as of a pomander; but the scent is subtle and curious enough to excite in us an eager desire to discover whence it comes, and as we join the scattered evidences together, the character of Burton himself slowly shapes into that of a wise, kindly, romantic man, a disappointed idealist who has begun, after the habit of his kind, to profess a cynicism he cannot maintain. Through the loopholes in his citadel of authorities, the intervals in his quotations from the satirists, his inveterate charity peeps out; he cannot disguise his faith that the purpose of education is to enable common human kindness to play its high part in the world, nor reconcile himself to the uselessness to which he is condemned. He is distressed by his own divorce from life, regretting not only that the university lights burn away in a sterile illumination of each other, but that they are also cut off from happiness by 'the laws and rigorous customs that forbid men to marry at set times and in some places, as apprentices, servants, collegiates'. Throughout his book this demon of regret lurks in the background. Burton, we feel, is precisely conscious of the futility of the huge labour of compiling it; it is not least his complete lack of all illusion about his own occupation which gives the *Anatomy* its faint but inimitable flavour and makes it not futile at all.

The *Anatomy* is not a bitter book, but it contains the harvest of much bitterness. There is something naïve in

Bishop Kennet's statement that Burton wrote it to cure
his melancholy but only made it worse, for the Bishop
was confounding cause and effect. The book and the
melancholy were both largely the outcome of his resentment against his destiny; it was hardly to be expected
that a man who had spent twenty or thirty years in
erecting a vast monument to his own pitiful lack of true
occupation would be made very merry by contemplating
the architecture of it. Conditions have changed at the
universities now, and it would be manifestly extravagant
to suggest that Burton was the archetype of the don;
but most Oxford and Cambridge men can remember
at least a few Fellows of an older generation who were
Burtons in miniature, with something of his inward rage
against his own futility, something of his learning, his
kindliness, his idealism, and something even of the sub-
acid resignation with which he accepted his fate and
made mock of it, as in his telling of the charming parable
from Plato:

'Now for poets, rhetoricians, historians, philosophers,
mathematicians, sophisters; they are like grasshoppers, sing
they must in the summer and pine in the winter, for there
is no preferment for them. Even so they were at first, if you
will believe that pleasant tale of Socrates, which he told fair
Phaedrus under a plane-tree, at the banks of the river Iseus;
about noon when it was hot, and the grasshoppers made
a noise, he took that sweet occasion to tell him a tale, how
grasshoppers were once scholars, musicians, poets, etc., before the Muses were born, and lived without meat and drink,
and for that cause were turned by Jupiter into grasshoppers.
And may be turned again, *In Tythoni Cicadas, aut Lyciorum
ranas*, for any reward I see they are like to have: or else in
the meantime, I would they could live as they did, without
any viaticum, like so many manucodiatae, those Indian
birds of paradise, as we commonly call them, those I mean

that live with the air and dew of heaven, and need no other
food. For being as they are, their rhetoric only serves them
to curse their bad fortunes, and many of them for want of
means are driven to hard shifts; from grasshoppers they turn
bumble-bees and wasps, plain parasites, and make the
muses, mules, to satisfy their hunger-starved paunches, and
get a meal's meat.'

No doubt Burton's profound depression had other
causes than his own sense of futility. He was born under
Mercury, and 'Mercurialists are solitary, much in contemplation, subtile, poets, philosophers, and musing
most part about such matters'; this might not have
mattered to another man, but Burton happened to
believe in the influence of the planets. An astrologer
who was born under a melancholy star could hardly
avoid being melancholy. Or is it we who are this time
confounding cause and effect, and did Burton first cast
his horoscope to find a reason for his own depression?
It was hardly necessary, for by his own confession the
misery of his schooldays was a quite sufficient cause.

'Parents and such as have the tuition and oversight of
children' (he wisely says) 'offend many times in that they
are too stern, always threatening, chiding, brawling, whip-
ping, or striking; by means of which their poor children are
so disheartened and cowed, that they never after have any
courage, a merry hour in their lives, or take pleasure in
any thing. There is great moderation to be had in such
things, as matters of great moment to the making or marring
of a child.'

The usher at the grammar school of Sutton Coldfield
probably had the first hand in marring Burton. 'Moped
many times weary of his life,' he lost the courage to
confront the world; he became a solitary, a romanticist,
a builder of castles in the air. No one was ever more

eager to see the curiosities of the world than he, but the only travels he dared to undertake were made among his books; there he indulged himself and voyaged, in the ethereal journey of his magnificent *Digression of the Air*, to the ends of earth; but it was a pathetic makeshift for a man born in those adventurous days.

In the language of modern psychology, Burton suffered under an inhibition; his nerve was shattered, and while he watched himself stagnating, chained by his fear of life to Oxford, his resentment against his destiny accumulated. At moments he looked upon himself as one prevented by the ill order of the world from exercising his true gifts, and cried, like Hamlet, that he lacked advancement. It was only partly true; he knew well enough, as many a disappointed don has known since his time, that he had played for safety and achieved it. The bitter knowledge worked 300 years ago as it does now; it made his depression deeper. It was deeper still because his practical gifts were great. There is nothing in the least fantastic about the remarkable Utopia which he describes in the huge preface to the sixth edition, published in 1651–2, twelve years after his death, a preface that has the substance of a dozen modern books; it is hardly a Utopia at all, but rather a detailed programme of enlightened social reform that any benevolent despot might have made a reality. First of all, he would have the wasteful common lands enclosed, 'yet not depopulated,' each peasant having his holding assigned by independent assessors; where no freehold was possible, the tenant should be guaranteed a long lease and a known rent; no taxes on imported necessaries; subsidized expeditions of discovery; commercial attachés appointed to the embassies abroad to note any improvement in the useful arts; public maintenance of public works, such as a copious water supply, hospitals for the sick, the old, and the indigent, fire-engines, cemeteries, colleges of mathematicians, musicians and actors, chemists, physicians, artists, and philosophers, 'that all arts and sciences may sooner be perfected and better learned,' free public schools for all where grammar and languages are taught not by the ordinary tedious precept, 'but by use, example, and conversation as travellers learn abroad'; public trustees, and a public supply of legal aid. But Burton was no egalitarian; his state was to be monarchical, and hereditary honours were to be permitted on condition that they could be freely acquired by men of merit, for he was fully convinced of the justice and expediency of the *carrière ouverte aux talents*. In the current phrase, he was for equality of opportunity.

'Once more, though thou be a barbarian, born at Ton-tonteac, a villain, a slave, a Saldanian negro, a seignior of Italy, I care not how descended, of what family, of what order, baron, count, prince, if thou be well qualified and he not, but a degenerate Neoptolemus, I must tell thee in a word, thou art a man, and he is a beast.'

And it scarcely becomes us of the present day to declare his idealism unpractical because he made no provision in his State for an army. His reasons for excluding soldiers (though he considered the condition of the world such that the ports and frontier towns, but no others, had better be fortified) have, alas! a curiously modern ring; it is likely to take society a good many centuries more to learn old Burton's lesson on the misery of war.

'Whilst the statesmen themselves in the meantime are secure at home pampered with all delights and pleasures, take their ease, and follow their lusts, not considering what intolerable misery poor soldiers endure, their often wounds, hunger, thirst, etc., the lamentable cares, torments, calamities, and oppressions that accompany such proceedings, they feel not, take no notice of it.'

The practical wisdom and humanity which are conspicuous in his Utopia are constant qualities of his book: superstitious though he was, his hatred of bigotry and intolerance was intense. All the absurdities and extravagances of the human race are exhibited against a background of kindliness and sympathy, seen through a charitable atmosphere that rises almost imperceptibly from the humane precepts he insinuates, and from his beloved habit of balancing extreme against extreme and censuring both. So in the matter of diet—the three doctors he really trusts, he says somewhere, are Dr. Merryman, Dr. Diet, and Dr. Quiet—he is impatient with the epicure: 'Lucullus's ghost walks still, and every man desires to sup with Apollo. . . . These Centaurs and Lapithae toss pots and bowls as so many balls; invent new tricks, as sausages, anchovies, tobacco, caviare, pickled oysters, herrings, fumadoes'—but he cannot approve those who affect 'a too ceremonious and strict diet, being over-precise, cockney-like, and curious in their observation of meats'.

On other questions he would sometimes carry his method of 'snarl and counter-snarl' (as Keats unkindly called it) to the point of appearing to blow hot and cold with the same breath, as in the matter of tobacco:

'Tobacco, divine, rare, and super-excellent tobacco, which goes far beyond all the panaceas, potable gold, and philosopher's stones, a sovereign remedy for all diseases. A good vomit, I confess, a virtuous herb, if it be well qualified, opportunely taken and medicinally used; but as it is commonly used by most men, which take it as workers do ale, 'tis a plague, a mischief, a violent purger of goods, land, health, hellish, devilish, and damned tobacco, the ruin and overthrow of body and soul.'

The final outcome of all his unwearied, infinitesimal pursuit of the remedy for melancholy, which is only another name for the secret of happiness, is that people should be rational, charitable, and imaginative. Nurses must not frighten children with tales of hobgoblins, nor fanatic preachers terrify grown men and women with thundering threats of everlasting damnation. This rejection of the terrifying sermon was nothing less than a self-denying ordinance, for Burton had not merely a general gift of vituperation but a particular genius for dwelling on hell fire. He suppressed it, however, for this little passage stands solitary in his book, though it is enough to show that he might have rivalled Donne in the kind:

'The terrible meditation of hell fire much torments a silly soul. What's a thousand years to eternity: *ubi moeror, ubi fletus, ubi dolor sempiternus. Mors sine morte, finis sine fine*; a finger burnt by chance we may not endure, the pain is so grievous, we may not abide an hour, a night is intolerable; and what shall this unspeakable fire be that burns for ever, innumerable infinite millions of years, *in omne aevum, in aeternum*. O eternity!'

As men must not be terrified by religion, they must not be tortured by convention. He advises other nations to avoid the extreme pangs of love-melancholy by follow-ing the liberal English custom of permitting 'our wives and daughters to go to the tavern with a friend'. At the last, like a benevolent uncle, after retailing all the vain remedies for the extremities of love-melancholy, he puts his hand in his pocket and brings all his good advice to a golden end: 'The last and surest remedy, to be put into practice in the utmost place when no other means will take effect, is to let them go together and enjoy each other.'

It is in this famous last section of his book on love-melancholy that Burton reveals himself most plainly as the romantic idealist. Though he claims that he is 'but a novice, a contemplator only, *Nescio quid sit amor nec amo*,' he has his own very positive preferences in this difficult matter of love. It is seldom indeed in the *Anatomy* that he speaks in his own person; in discussing love he does so three times. He vigorously applauds three actions, and they are three marriages, and—what is more—three marriages of the same fairy-tale kind. First, 'Great Alexander married Roxane a poor man's child, only for her person. 'Twas well done of Alexander, and heroically done. I admire him for it.' Here are the other two:

'Leontius, a philosopher of Athens, had a fair daughter called Athenias, *multo corporis lepore ac Venere* (saith mine author), of a comely carriage, he gave her no portion but her bringing up, *occulto formae presagio*, out of some secret foreknowledge of her fortune, bestowing that little which he had amongst his other children. But she, thus qualified, was preferred by some friends to Constantinople, to serve Pulcheria, the emperor's sister, of whom she was baptized and called Eudocia. Theodosius, the emperor, in short space took notice of her excellent beauty and good parts, and a little after, upon his sister's sole commendation made her his wife: 'twas nobly done of Theodosius. Rodophe was the fairest lady in her days in all Egypt; she went to wash her, and by chance (her maids meanwhile looking but carelessly to her clothes) an eagle stole away one of her shoes, and laid it in Psammeticus the King of Egypt's lap at Memphis: he wondered at the excellency of the shoe and pretty foot, but more *Aquilae factum*, at the manner of the bringing of it: and caused forthwith proclamation to be made, that she that owned the shoe should come presently to his Court; the virgin came, and was forthwith married to the king. I say this was heroically done, and like a prince; I commend him for it, and all such as have means, that will either do (as he did) themselves, or so for love, etc., marry their children.'

So we think of this old scholar as a fairy godfather, with his visions of mankind made prosperous and happy, eating his heart out in his rooms at Christ Church, for the lack of opportunity to put the world right by a wave of his wand, rummaging through pile after pile of dusty folios in the full knowledge that the end would only be to add one of the largest to the vast array. What solace he found for his depression, save to hear the bargees swearing, we cannot easily discover. Perhaps he derived happiness from sharing the belief of Marguerite of Navarre that 'l'ennui est commun à toute personne bien née'; he certainly believed, as a whole phalanx of romantics have since believed, that depression is the mark of intellectual distinction. 'I am (he says) of that nobleman's mind, "Melancholy advanceth men's conceits, more than any other humour whatsoever," improves their meditations more than any strong drink or sack.' The compilation of the *Anatomy* did not help him much: his fishing, we are sure, was not done at Oxford, nor his boating—'to take a boat in a pleasant evening and with music to row upon the waters, which Plutarch so much applauds, Elian admires upon the river Pineus in those Thessalian fields'—on any mortal stream; and even the comfort of wine was denied him. 'Let's drive down care with a cup of wine; and so say I too (though *I drink none* myself).' We must believe his own italics, though they are hard to reconcile with his remedy against sleeplessness and bad dreams. 'Piso commends frications.

E

Andrew Borde a good draught of strong drink before one goes to bed: I say, a nutmeg and ale, or a good draught of muscadine, with a toast and nutmeg or a posset of the same, which many use in a morning, but methinks for such as have dry brains are much more proper at night.' With wine away, nothing seems left to console him, except a nutmeg and ale and that pleasant smoke of juniper which 'Bessardus Bisantinus prefers to melancholy persons, which is in great request with us at Oxford, to sweeten our chambers.'

That Burton suffered torments no one can doubt, in spite of the well-known passage in which he paints with delight the pleasures of the voluntary solitariness which 'gently brings on like a syren, a shoeing horn, or a sphinx to this irrevocable gulf'. *Facilis descensus Averno*; his descent to the depths was easy, but whether it was as delightful as he there describes it, whether indeed he went by that flowery path at all, is open to suspicion. This cry at least comes straight from a soul in pain: 'If there is a hell on earth, it is to be found in a melancholy man's heart. . . . I say of our melancholy man, he is the cream of human adversity, the quintessence, the upshot.' Yet it is strange that with all his reading—and he did not despise the vernacular—he should never have made contact with those tormented spirits who were putting forth their melancholy into plays for the London stage. *Hamlet* indeed, in which Burton would have found much to his liking, was actually played at Oxford; it is a pity he did not see it, for Shakespeare would have become to him more than the 'elegant' author of *Venus and Adonis* and *Much Ado about Nothing*. Had he followed up the acquaintance in the Folio he would not have had to let his sentence, 'A black man is a pearl in a fair woman's eye,' go unsupported by an instance as he did.

Perhaps the savage torment of Webster and Tourneur would have repelled as much as fascinated him; though their melancholy was well worth the anatomizing. Certainly he would have found Ford curiously congenial, not only because he was always 'deep in dump' and wore 'a melancholy hat', but because he shared Burton's almost childish tenderness and romanticism, as well as his habit of solitariness. Donne, too, even though he was to become one of the forbidden thundering preachers, would have interested him.

But it is evident that Burton went to his contemporaries, as dons nowadays go to novels, solely for pleasure and distraction. Shakespeare was to him only 'an elegant poet of ours'. Of Ben Jonson he knew only *Volpone* and *Every Man out of His Humour*, and a version from Catullus; he had read Marlowe's *Hero and Leander*; he was more familiar with Drayton and Daniel, though he commends neither. The *Faerie Queen* he knew well, and Spenser was to him 'our modern Maro'. But of all the English poets the one whom he read with surpassing relish and quoted with pre-eminent affection was 'our English Homer', 'Sir Geoffrey Chaucer'. Burton had the Canterbury Tales at his finger-ends, and he knew the *Wife of Bath* even better than his Virgil. We can guess the reason why. He recognized in Chaucer the shrewd humanity which he too shared, but in Chaucer tempered and perfected by a knowledge of life at first hand; the Canterbury pilgrims were substantial men and women out of busy highways, not dim figures of classical legend. In touching them Burton found something of the contact with the actual world which was denied him by his adverse star.

Thus, in making a reckoning of the positive pleasures of the old Oxford solitary, we should place the reading of Sir Geoffrey almost at the head; 'divine Seneca' was a pale ghost beside the English Homer of flesh and blood. Before this would come only the joy of writing those portions of the *Anatomy* in which he let himself fairly go. At his best Burton wrote a splendidly virile prose; he had the knack of turning epigrammatic Latin into still terser and more vigorous English, and he could do it with a flowing pen. '*Sicuti titulis primi fuere, sic et vitiis* (as they were first in rank, so in rottenness).' 'Malt-worms, men-fishes, or water-snakes, *qui bibunt solum more ranarum, nihil comedentes*, like so many frogs in a puddle.' The heaviest of his pages sparkles with such sentences. His cumulative effects (as in the well-known diatribe on women) are prodigious; he was always ready to gallop off with the dictionary thundering behind him. 'His soul was soused, imparadised, imprisoned in his lady.' ''Tis an inevitable chance, the first statute in Magna Charta, an everlasting Act of Parliament, all must die.' He loved words for their own sake, and he had the faculty, essential to the finest literary style, of making the spiritual physical by precipitating it, often with a violent jerk, into a concrete image.

It is, of course, mere folly to wish that Burton had written other books than the *Anatomy*, or the *Anatomy* otherwise; had he not written that book he would have written nothing. He made it, in spite of the myriad authorities he accumulates, after his own image: out of all his folios he managed to build a house which his spirit could comfortably inhabit, hidden away by many leathern doors and recondite passages from the gaze of the curious vulgar. There in the centre of the labyrinth he is to be found, wise, tender, romantic, sensitive, and charitable, hopelessly at odds with a world of which he was afraid. He is a little hard to know, but those who have the patience to persevere with his acquaintance can find for him no readier epithet than lovable; 'a person', says Antony Wood, 'of great honesty, plain dealing, and charity.' The time of his popularity is long past; we no longer need to ransack the classics, or be saved labour of ransacking them, in order to buttress our lightest word with authority. Still, it is likely that those who used him most cared for him least, for it is not in man's nature to cherish a personal affection for the editor of an encyclopaedia from which he steals. We of the present day, who have no ulterior motive in seeking him out, but frequent him solely for our own delight, may have the privilege of knowing and loving Robert Burton for his own sake alone.   [MARCH 1921.

IV

THE POETRY OF WILLIAM COLLINS

'THOU diedst, a most rare boy, of melancholy,' said Belarius over the unconscious body of Imogen-Fidele. It may have been the fascination of a fate that he felt so like his own which allured Collins to make the courageous but strange attempt to compose another dirge in place of the incomparable—

> Fear no more the heat of the sun
> Nor the furious winter's rages.

His attempt was, as it was bound to be, a failure; nor is it really a very interesting failure except to those who seek for what clues they can find to the baffling achievement of a poet whose work, though he lived miserably for thirteen years after, was finished at the age of twenty-four.

We must suppose that Collins's *Dirge for Cymbeline*, first printed in 1749, was one of his last poems, if not the very last; and we are surprised that he was then farther removed from the Shakespearian simplicity he coveted than he had been as a schoolboy of seventeen.[1]

> Young Damon of the vale is dead,
>   Ye lowly hamlets, moan;
> A dewy turf lies o'er his head,
>   And at his feet a stone,

is nearer to perfection of the kind he sought than is—

> To fair Fidele's grassy tomb
>   Soft maids and village hinds shall bring
> Each opening sweet of earliest bloom
>   And rifle all the breathing spring.

[1] See note, p. 190.

The line of *Cymbeline* on which the verse is based—

> With fairest flowers
> While summer lasts and I live here, Fidele,
> I'll sweeten thy sad grave——

is fatal to Collins's adaptation. It is not that his dirge has no qualities of its own. It is musical, almost limpid. But it is weak; the emotional impulse is not concentrated and embodied. It visibly trickles away through the porous vessel of poetic commonplace. In *Cymbeline* Shakespeare himself was sometimes not very far removed from that condition of relaxed control; but concentration was too deep an instinct with him ever to be quite forgotten. 'I'll sweeten thy sad grave' is tense and over-flowing in a manner of which he could never wholly lose, and Collins could never—save in one immortal poem—wholly gain the mastery.

We know little of Collins, and the reticence of his poetry is such as makes us feel that even if we knew much more, it would be knowledge of the kind that is irrelevant. His poetry indicates that he was a man pre-occupied with his art, and it is easy to imagine that a contributing cause to his final and fatal melancholia was a morbid sense of dissatisfaction with his own work. He was engrossed in it, as far as he could be engrossed in anything; the activity of his mind seems to have been wholly focused upon poetic achievement, and his sensibility seems to have been determined chiefly by his hopes and fears as a poet. At least one half of the Odes in the 1746 volume are addressed to personified emotions to which he aspires to give poetic expression—Fear, Pity, the Passions—to the Manners he longs to represent, or the Poetical Character he desires to emulate. Nothing could more clearly reveal the self-conscious literary artist, for whom his own activity is already become an obsession.

The danger of this intense concentration upon a purely literary purpose is an impoverishment of the sensibility. The emotions and perceptions which are the raw material of literature are not themselves aesthetic; they are just ordinary emotions and perceptions, but felt with a keener particularity than those of ordinary men, and often felt when the ordinary man feels nothing at all. The aesthetic emotion supervenes only in the process of projecting them into words which will compel another to feel them again. To accumulate these emotions and perceptions in their proper intensity demands an instinctive abandonment, a complete surrender to experience, of which the self-conscious literary artist becomes less capable as his obsession with his art grows upon him. The aesthetic impulse emerges too soon; it insists on guiding and determining perceptions which can only be profound if they are independent; and in extreme cases it ends by interposing a veil between the artist and the reality, and perpetually prevents the life-giving contact between his sensibility and the unique experiences upon which the significance of his art depends. When Trigorin, in Tchehov's *Seagull*, had reached the point at which he could not see a cloud without immediately saying: 'That cloud is like a piano', he recognized in himself the symptoms of literary decrepitude. A rich creative nature does not need to label its perceptions on the wing; if you stick a pin through a butterfly it dies. Only the nervous and insecure writer feels that he cannot afford to wait.

If at this point of time we are to be scrupulously just to Collins, we must recognize in his work a sensibility overweighted from the beginning by a precocious literary instinct. The very perfection of the two schoolboy poems that have come down to us—'Young Damon of the vale

is dead' and 'When Phoebe formed a wanton smile'—
is disturbing, for they show that the aesthetic impulse
had reached the highest point of acuteness long before
the sensibility could have established any real contact
with experience at all. Those two poems are not excellent imitations; they are perfect achievements. We
could put the Phoebe 'sonnet' among the best work of
the minor Carolines, and it would easily hold its place.

> When Phœbe formed a wanton smile,
>   My soul! it reached not here!
> Strange that thy peace, thou trembler, flies
>   Before a rising tear!
> From midst the drops my love is born,
>   That o'er those eyelids rove;
> Thus issued from a teeming wave
>   The fabled queen of love.

It is only because they happen to know it was the
work of a schoolboy that the editors of the anthologies
exclude it. And the same is true of *Young Damon*.
Remove the backstairs knowledge of its date and origin,
and it would be accepted as a perfect thing of its kind,
exquisite in music, beautiful in diction. If we put the
evidence of this altogether precocious sense of form
together with the self-conscious literary impulse which
reveals itself in the majority of the Odes, we see Collins
as a man prematurely burdened with a gift of deliberate
poetic expression, one whose sensibility could hardly fail
to be deadened by the aesthetic preoccupation interposed
between it and direct experience. He was prevented from
feeling by the impatience of his intense desire to feel.

> O thou, whose spirit most possessed
> The sacred seat of Shakespeare's breast!
> By all that from thy prophet broke,
> In thy divine emotions spoke;

Hither again thy fury deal,
Teach me but once like him to feel. . . .

So he importunes Fear; but he asks the same thing from
Pity. 'There let me oft, retired by day, In dreams of
passion melt away.' Or he calls to Nature, 'If but from
thee I hope to feel . . .'

It is the perennial cry of the starved sensibility, impotent to break through the barriers raised by its own
devouring instinct for artistic perfection. It seems that
Collins could have expressed anything, so rich was his
technical endowment; yet that endowment came near
preventing him from having anything to express at all.
One perfect poem, and one only, lifts him out of the
ranks of the minor poets; he can only just support the
posthumous renown heaped upon him by a tradition
of criticism which is unduly impatient of Pope and the
Augustans. Collins brings a breath of a diviner fragrance, it has been said over and over again; but is it—
save in the one great poem—really more divine? To
safeguard ourselves against an ecstasy of wonder at this
phoenix in the desert of the eighteenth century, we need
to remember—what is too easily forgotten—what Pope
could do and did, to reconsider for a moment passages
such as these two from *The Unfortunate Lady*:

Most souls, 'tis true, but peep out once an age,
Dull sullen prisoners in the body's cage:
Dim lights of life, that burn a length of years,
Useless, unseen, as lamps in sepulchres;
Like Eastern kings a lazy state they keep
And close confined to their own palace sleep . . .

What tho' no sacred earth allow thee room,
Nor hallow'd dirge be uttered o'er thy tomb?
Yet shall thy grave with rising flowers be dressed
And the green turf lie lightly on thy breast:

> There shall the morn her earliest tears bestow,
> There the first roses of the year shall blow;
> While angels with their silver wings o'ershade
> The ground now sacred by thy reliques made . . .

The second of these passages is on a favourite theme of
Collins. It appears in the *Dirge for Cymbeline*, in the *Ode
to Thomson*, in the stanzas to the memory of Colonel Ross,
and in *How sleep the Brave*. But only in the last does
Collins achieve an expression that is equal to Pope's.
In the *Ode to Thomson*, for instance, he writes:

> The year's best sweets shall duteous rise
>   To deck its poet's sylvan grave.

That is really almost as far from Pope's couplet, 'Yet
shall thy grave', as it is from Shakespeare's 'I'll sweeten
thy sad grave'. It is on an altogether different plane.
In *How Sleep the Brave*, it is true, Collins reaches the level
of Pope in his handling of the theme.

> When spring with dewy fingers cold
> Returns to deck their hallowed mould,
> She there shall dress a sweeter sod
> Than fancy's feet have ever trod.

Perhaps the purity of the phrase 'with dewy fingers cold'
lifts those lines by an almost imperceptible degree above
the lines of Pope; but it is the fraction of a degree, no
more. In treating the commonplace of nature Pope and
Collins were on a level. But the earlier lines we have
quoted from *The Unfortunate Lady*, 'Most souls, 'tis
true . . .' are of a kind and excellence beyond Collins's
range. They touch the intensity and psychological
revelation of Donne, and have a sustained perfection of
phrasing that Donne never attained.

We may crudely state the relative position thus: if we
take away from Collins the *Ode to Evening*, his remaining

excellence would be comfortably contained in a third
of Pope's excellence, for besides the commonplace of
Nature, Pope was also a master of Wit in the best
Metaphysical sense—namely, the striking expression of
deep psychological perceptions, the power which could

> the deep knowledge of dark truths so teach
> That sense might judge what fancy could not reach—

and of wit in the Augustan sense, the verbal epigram of
an extraordinarily alert mind. Had the *Ode to Evening*
by some malevolent dispensation never existed, no one
would now be calling *How Sleep the Brave* a great poem.
It is, indeed, a perfect poem; but there are very many
perfect poems of the same scope in the English language,
and Collins would have slipped quietly into an honour-
able but seldom remembered place among their authors.
Only the specialist would have occupied himself with
looking through those of his pieces which were not in
the anthologies, and perhaps even the specialist, no
longer forewarned of the quality to look for, would have
missed the scattered lines through which the reverbera-
tion of a more solemn music is heard.

> Or in some hollow seat
> 'Gainst which the big waves beat
> Hear drowning seamen's cries in tempests brought . . .

> Happier hopeless fair if never
> Her baffled hands with vain endeavour
> Had touched that fatal zone to her denied . . .

> The band, as fairy legends say,
> Was wove on that creating day
> When He, who called with thought to birth
> Yon tented sky, this laughing earth
> And dressed with springs and forests tall
> And poured the main engirting all . . .

Such things as these, which point more directly than the minor perfection of *How Sleep the Brave* towards the *Ode to Evening*, would make us feel that if only he had something to say, some deeply felt experience to crystallize, the great poem might come; but it would be a possibility and no more. For if the purity and resonance of these scattered lines is remarkable, the taste, which in the schoolboy was almost impeccable, is now a prey to the strangest aberrations. In spite of his sincere, conscious, and passionate pursuit of simplicity, Collins seems to have suffered as much as any one from the rhetorical *mièvrerie* of the period. Sheer lapses of taste are much more frequent in his poems than one cares to remember ; and, as Hazlitt said, he is sometimes affected, unmeaning, and obscure.[1] True, one of the most strangely beautiful verses of the *Ode to Evening* is obscure; and if Collins had been more often obscure after this fashion there would be nothing to complain of. But a far more characteristic kind of obscurity in his poetry seems to be the result of a deficiency as much in power of thought as in urgency of feeling. And even though Collins was a good classical scholar and his love of the Greek was one of the chief influences in his idealization of Simplicity, who comes,

a decent maid
In Attic robe arrayed,

he seems at the crucial moment to be insensitive to the difference between Greek clarity and English diffuseness and obscurity. When he wrote, 'The fiend of Nature joined his yoke', he was not writing English at all, but the jargon of a classical crib; and there is still more

[1] See note, p. 190.

striking evidence of this blind spot in his mind in the *Ode to Liberty*.

> O Goddess, in that feeling hour
> When most its sounds should court thy ears,
> Let not my shell's misguided power
> E'er draw thy sad, thy mindful tears.

At the bottom of the page Collins printed the line from Callimachus' *Hymn to Demeter*, of which his four lines are an expansion,

> Μὴ μὴ ταῦτα λέγωμες ἃ δάκρυον ἄγαγε Δηοῖ

By the side of that lovely line Collins's are unmitigated stucco; and it is curiously revealing that he could print them on the page together. At the end of the same ode—to close the account of Collins's insensitiveness— he borrows from a writer who was to him no less than a classic, from Milton.

> Her let our Sires and Matrons hoar
> Welcome to Britain's ravaged shore,
> Our youths, enamoured of the fair,
> Play with the tangles of her hair.

To apply to Liberty, the Lady who shall rule the West, the phrase which Milton used of those who preferred the company of Amaryllis and Neæra to the last infirmity of noble mind—*curiosa infelicitas!*

This is not to say that Collins's aberrations were very peculiar in that somewhat rococo age. Thomson, who had a very considerable influence upon him, had many similar vices of taste. But, to compensate, he had a creative vitality which could carry them along on its stream; and, to excuse, he had not the classical scholarship of Collins. It is Collins's perceptible striving after classical simplicity, as much as the tenuity of his content, which makes his lapses appear catastrophes. Possibly we ought to put the insecurity of his judgement to the direct account of Thomson, whose intimate friend he had become during the year that preceded the publication of the *Odes*; but if we do this we ought in fairness also to ascribe to Thomson the deepening of content, the sudden breaking through the closed circle of purely literary perceptions which distinguishes the *Ode to Evening* from the rest of his work. Certainly it was not from Thomson that Collins acquired his sense of form, which came from the classics and Milton, but from Thomson rather than Milton he derived his use of thinly-disguised and awkward latinisms, his 'decent' and 'frequent'. Nevertheless, the evidence is that, on the whole, Thomson's influence upon Collins was quite as much good as bad. 'Thomson was an inspired poet,' said Wordsworth, 'but he could not work miracles: in cases where the art of seeing had in some degree been learned, the teacher would further the proficiency of his pupils, but he could do no more.' It was precisely this 'art of seeing' that Collins seems to have learned from him, and it is likely that Thomson gave more than he got in the exchange, though in the passage which Collins directly borrowed from Thomson, he in a certain sense improved on his original. Thomson had written in *Winter*,

> In vain for him the officious wife prepares
> The fire fair-blazing and the vestment warm;
> In vain his little children, peeping out
> Into the mingling storm, demand their sire
> With tears of artless innocence. . . .

In *Popular Superstitions of the Highlands* Collins transforms this into

> For him, in vain, the anxious wife shall wait
>   Or wander forth to meet him on his way;

> For him, in vain, at to-fall of the day
> His babes shall linger at the unclosing gate.

And Gray was almost certainly working over the same original in the familiar lines,

> For them no more the blazing hearth shall burn,
> Or busy housewife ply her evening care:
> No children run to lisp their sire's return
> Or climb his knees the envied kiss to share.

A comparison of the three versions is interesting.[1] The Thomson is weak, but it is particular; he does put a picture before us. Gray at once generalizes it, and makes the stanza more resonant. Collins seems to pause half-way; he half generalizes; his verse is limpid, but it does not reverberate. It is a perilous kind of purity that he has achieved; it hovers on the verge of emptiness.

Nevertheless it is characteristic of Collins. He was deficient in the faculty of direct perception which best provides the material necessary if the technical process (even the most perfect) is not to operate idly in the void; he was deficient in the vigour of mind essential to the fresh apprehension and memorable utterance of great commonplace. That he should have snatched a victory from between these two deficiencies seems almost miraculous. But it was not altogether a miracle. A comparison of the *Ode on Colonel Ross* and *How Sleep the Brave* shows how much labour went to the making of the perfect little poem, for the *Ode* is hardly more than a diffuse preliminary version of the poem. Here are the relevant passages of the *Ode*.

> That sacred spot the village hind
> With every sweetest turf shall bind
>   And peace protect the shade. . . .
> Aerial hands shall build thy tomb . . .

[1] See note, p. 190.

While Honour bathed in tears shall rove
To sigh thy name thro' every grove
   And call his heroes round. . . .

But lo! where sunk in deep despair
Her garments torn, her bosom bare,
   Impatient Freedom lies,
Her matted tresses madly spread,
To every sod, which wraps the dead,
   She turns her joyless eyes.

In those lines are the rough-hewn originals of almost every line in the finished poem.

How sleep the brave, who sink to rest
By all their country's wishes blest,
When Spring with dewy fingers cold
Returns to deck their hallowed mould,
She there shall dress a sweeter sod
Than Fancy's feet have ever trod.

By fairy hands their knell is rung,
By forms unseen their dirge is sung;
There Honour comes, a pilgrim gray,
To bless the turf that wraps their clay;
And Freedom shall awhile repair
To dwell a weeping hermit there.

At last, though with no added richness of perception, Collins had controlled his materials. The rhetoric is subdued to reticence; he has achieved the simplicity of a fine Greek epigram.

To carry Collins beyond this point, which, though it is a pinnacle, is a pinnacle of minor poetry, not more art but more seeing and feeling were necessary. And, for the great occasion, they came. Throughout the *Ode to Evening* the epithets are no longer worn; they are exact and revealing, the imperishable symbols of a unique perception.

Like thy own brawling springs,
Thy springs and dying gales . . .

If he takes over from Milton, together with the marvellous verse-form from the version of *Quis multa gracilis*,
the older poet's line, 'What time the gray-fly winds her
sultry horn', it is to give the phrase a fresh and appro-
priate precision.

Or where the beetle winds
His small but sullen horn.

And we may watch his effort to get rid of the vague
rhetoric of Gothic romanticism and supply its place with
that magical evocation of emotion which is contained
in the thing seen.

Then let me rove some wild and heathy scene
Or find some ruin midst its dreary dells,
    Whose walls more awful nod
    By thy religious gleams

gives way to the obscurely precise and (save perhaps
for 'sheety') wholly exquisite

Then lead, calm votaress, where some sheety lake
Cheers the lone heath, or some time-hallowed pile,
    Or upland fallows gray
    Reflect its last cool gleam.

And as if to prove how deliberate was his art, and how
certain his judgement when he was no longer trying to
create out of the void, in a single verse he incorporates
one of Thomson's most beautiful epithets and the finest
phrase of his own *How Sleep the Brave*.

Views wilds and swelling floods
And hamlets brown and dim-discovered spires
And hears their simple bell, and marks o'er all
    Thy dewy fingers draw
    The gradual dusky veil.

'Dewy fingers' is his own; 'dim-discovered' comes from
a passage in Thomson's *Summer*, in itself very beautiful,
of which we can see the peculiar attraction for Collins's
contemplative melancholy.

> Unhappy he! who from the first of joys,
> Society, cut off, is left alone
> Amid this world of death! Day after day
> Sad on the jutting eminence he sits
> And views the main that ever toils below
> Still fondly forming in the farthest verge
> Where the round ether mixes with the wave
> Ships, dim-discovered, dropping from the clouds.

But both Thomson's phrase and his own are recreated,
set in a new relation, and given a new potency; they
are recharged with perceptual emotion. Even the one
phrase in the poem which at the first glance seems
almost archaistic—'With brede ethereal wove'—afterwards appears as the successful culmination of other
attempts to use an image which fascinated him.

> All the shadowy tribes of mind
> In braided dance their murmurs joined. . . .

> Beyond yon braided clouds that lie
> Paving the light-embroidered sky. . . .

But to expound the beauties of the *Ode to Evening* is
superfluous. It is a perfect and a great poem. For the
one and only time Collins's sensibility was brought into
direct contact with a profound experience; for the one
and only time he had a deep and particular emotion to
recollect in tranquillity, on the embodiment of which
he could fitly lavish his art. He had no need to fear the
remembered beauties of other poets, for on this occasion
the content of his own mind was definite and urgent
enough to compel them to submit to his purpose, to
abandon their old allegiance and accept his own.

We may regard Collins as an example of the triumphs and dangers of the pursuit of style. Without the apparatus of a perfect technique he would never have been able to build so complete and final a memorial of the emotion which overwhelmed him when at the last it came; but the adequacy of his preparation for it almost scared it away. We might speculate for long and in vain on the question whether he gained or lost on the whole. Were there no *Ode to Evening* we might confidently say he lost: but that one poem changes everything. We feel that it is the complete and exhaustive expression of a sensibility. A hundred imperfectly realized poems could not balance it in the scale; and there are moments when we are inclined to say that it alone outweighs the whole production of Thomson's richer nature. He, with many times the ore, lacked the power to refine any of it completely; from a single piece, Collins made a poem of pure gold. The pursuit of style is a perilous thing; but without it there is no permanence. 'On ne vit que par le style', as Chateaubriand said, for style is the name we give to the specific transmutation of the sensibility into the created thing. It is the condition of immortality, and it is the cause that to-day, for one person who reads Thomson's *Seasons*, there are a hundred who have read and cannot forget the *Ode to Evening*.   [NOVEMBER 1921.

V

THE POETRY OF JOHN CLARE

IN 1820 Messrs. Taylor & Hessey published two books
whose immediate renown was in singular contrast
with their after-fame. *Poems Descriptive of Rural Life and
Scenery*, by John Clare, a Northamptonshire Peasant,
ran into four editions within a year; the five hundred
copies of the single edition of *Lamia, Isabella, and other
Poems*, by John Keats, were not exhausted till the
'forties. Clare's popularity dwindled gradually into
complete neglect; he had been all but wholly forgotten
by the time that Monckton Milnes assumed the practical
task of impressing upon the world the conviction of the
poets that Keats was among the greatest. Quickly the
labours of piety were accomplished; within a few years
Keats's poetical remains were gathered together, until
nothing substantial remained to be added. Clare went
on writing indefatigably in the exile of an asylum for
nearly thirty years after he had been forgotten, and not
till to-day have two young poets set themselves to the
task of rescuing all that is valuable in his work.[1]

It is not merely because the year and the publishers
were the same that we are drawn to think of Keats and
Clare together. The association of the great name and
the small one has a curious congruity. Keats and Clare
both suffered 'a vast shipwreck of their life's esteems',
the one sudden and intolerably tragic, the other lingering and not without a sunset-haze of vaguely remembered happiness. There were elements common to their
characters—they were both parvenus in the ranks of

---

[1] JOHN CLARE: POEMS: Chiefly from Manuscript. Selected and
Edited by *Edmund Blunden* and *Alan Porter*.

men of letters, and they shared a resolution and an independence which became almost intolerant; Keats had an unusual, and Clare a unique knowledge of country sights and sounds; the most perfect poem of each is an *Ode to Autumn*.

We are inclined to lay stress on the points of resemblance in order that the cardinal point of difference may more plainly appear; for the eagerness with which we welcome this collection of Clare's poetry is likely to be so genuine and so justified as to disturb our sense of proportion. Into a generation of poets who flirt with nature suddenly descends a true nature-poet, one whose intimate and self-forgetful knowledge of the ways of birds and beasts and flowers rises like the scent of open fields from every page. Surely the only danger is that the enthusiasm of our recognition may be excessive; the relief overpowering with which we greet a poet who not only professes, but proves by the very words of his profession, that his dream of delight is

> To note on hedgerow baulks, in moisture sprent
>   The jetty snail creep from the mossy thorn,
> With earnest heed and tremulous intent,
>   Frail brother of the morn,
> That from the tiny bents and misted leaves
>   Withdraws his timid horn,
>   And fearful vision weaves.

We have indeed almost to be on our guard against the sweet, cool shock of such a verse; the emotional quality is so assured and individual, the language so simple and inevitable, the posture of mind so unassuming and winning, that one is tempted for a moment to believe that while Wordsworth was engaged in putting the poetry of nature wrong by linking it to a doubtful metaphysic, John Clare was engaged in putting it right.

And so in a sense it was. As a poet of nature Clare
was truer, more thoroughly subdued to that in which
he worked than Wordsworth. Wordsworth called upon
the poet to keep his eye upon the object; but his eye was
hardly so penetrating and keen as Clare's. Yet Wordsworth was a great poet, and Keats, with whom Clare's
kinship was really closer, was a great poet, and Clare
was not; and it is important in the case of a poet whose
gifts and qualities are so enchanting as Clare's are to
bear in mind from the outset the vital difference between them. Wordsworth belongs to another sphere
than Clare in virtue of the range of his imaginative
apprehension: Keats in virtue not only of his imagination, but also of his art. In one respect Clare was a finer
artist than Wordsworth, he had a truer ear and a more
exquisite instinct for words; but he had nothing of the
principle of inward growth which gives to Wordsworth's
most careless work a place within the unity of a great
scheme. Wordsworth's incessant effort to comprehend
experience would itself have been incomprehensible to
Clare; Keats's consuming passion to make his poetry
adequate not merely in content but also in the very
mechanism of expression to an emotional experience
more overwhelming even than Wordsworth's would
have seemed to him like a problem of metaphysics to
a ploughboy.

Clare was indeed a singer born. His nature was
strangely simple, and his capacity for intense emotion
appears at first sight to have been almost completely
restricted to a response to nature. The intensity with
which he adored the country that he knew is without
a parallel in English literature; of him it seems hardly
a metaphor to say he was an actual part of his countryside. Away from it he pined; he became queer and

irresponsible. With his plants and birds and bees and fields he was among his own people. The spiked thistle, the firetail, the hare, the white-nosed and the grand-father bee were his friends. Yet he hardly humanized them; he seems rather to have lived on the same level of existence as they, and to have known them as they know each other. We feel that it is only by an effort that he manages to make himself conscious of his emotion towards them or of his own motive in singing of it. In those rare moments he conceives of the voice of Nature as something eternal, outlasting all generations of men, whispering to them to sing also. Thus, while he sits under the huge old elm which is the shepherd's tree, listening to 'the laugh of summer leaves above',

> The wind of that eternal ditty sings,
> Humming of future things that burn the mind
> To leave some fragment of itself behind.

That is the most imaginative statement Clare ever made of his own poetic purpose. He, the poet, is one more of Nature's voices; and the same thought or the same instinct underlies the most exquisite of his earlier poems, *Song's Eternity*, a precious discovery of his present editors:

> Mighty songs that miss decay,
>   What are they?
> Crowds and cities pass away
>   Like a day.
> Books are out and books are read;
>   What are they?
> Years will lay them with the dead—
>   Sigh, sigh;
> Trifles unto nothing wed,
>   They die.

Dreamers, mark the honey bee,
  Mark the tree
Where the bluecap *tootle-tee*
  Sings a glee
Sung to Adam and to Eve—
  Here they be.
When floods covered every bough
  Noah's ark
Heard that ballad singing now;
  Hark, hark,

Tootle tootle tootle tee.
  Can it be
Pride and fame must shadows be?
  Come and see—
Every season owns her own;
  Bird and bee
Sing creation's music on;
  Nature's glee
Is in every mood and tone
  Eternity.

In many ways that is the most perfect of Clare's poems;
it has a poetic unity of a kind that he attained but
seldom, for in it are naturally combined the highest
apprehension of which Clare was capable and the
essential melody of his pre-eminent gift of song. It is
at once an assertion and an emotional proof of the
enduringness of the voice of Nature. Clare does not,
like the modern poet who has chosen the same theme,
adduce the times and the seasons and thereby challenge
the evolutionary theory; his history is the history of
myth. Not the Neanderthal man but Adam and Eve
heard the bluecap's same immortal song; for it is not
the fact, but the sense of song's eternity that the poet
has to give us. Clare does it triumphantly. Moreover,
in this poem, which we believe must henceforward take

its place by right in every anthology of English poetry, Clare achieved that final perfection of form which was so often to elude him. The bird-note begins, rises, dies away: and the poem is finished.

Clare's music was a natural music; as with Shelley's skylark, his art was unpremeditated and his strains profuse. He was perhaps never to find a form which fitted his genius so intimately as that of *Song's Eternity*. His language was to become more coherent and more vivid; but the inward harmony that is essential to a great poem was too often to escape him. He was like a child so intoxicated with his wonderful gift for whistling and his tune that he whistles it over and over again. The note is so pure, the tune so full of delight that we can never be tired; we listen to it as we listen to the drowsy enchantment of the monotony of sounds on a summer's afternoon, for it is as authentic and as sweet as they. The eternity of song was in Clare's blood; and when he recurs to the theme of enduring nature in simple stanzas,

> Some sing the pomps of chivalry
>   As legends of the ancient time,
> Where gold and pearls and mystery
>   Are shadows painted for sublime;
>
> But passions of sublimity
>   Belong to plain and simpler things,
> And David underneath a tree
>   Sought when a shepherd Salem's springs,
>
> Where moss did into cushions spring,
>   Forming a seat of velvet hue,
> A small unnoticed trifling thing
>   To all but heaven's hailing dew.

And David's crown hath passed away,
    Yet poesy breathes his shepherd skill,
His palace lost—and to this day
    The little moss is blossoming still,

we feel that here, too, is a music that need never end.

Clare's difficulty as a poet, in fact, can and ought to
be put baldly; he did not know when to stop. Why,
indeed, should he stop? He was either a voice, one of
the unending voices of Nature, or he was an eye, an
unwearied eye watching the infinite process of Nature;
perhaps never a poet consciously striving by means of
art to arouse in men's minds an emotion like his own.
All the art he had was that which he gained from his
recollection of other poets' tunes; the structure of their
harmony eluded him, he remembered only the melody.
Take, for instance, his extremely beautiful *Autumn*: the
melody comes directly from Collins's famous *Ode*; yet
how greatly Clare enriches it, as though with a material
golden stain of autumn! The last leaf seems to be falling
at our feet, the last bee zooming in our ears.

    Heart-sickening for the silence that is thine,
    Not broken inharmoniously as now
        That lone and vagrant bee
        Booms faint with weary chime.

    Now filtering winds thin winnow through the woods
    In tremulous noise that bids at every breath
        Some sickly cankered leaf
        Let go its hold, and die.

Not only these, but any one of a dozen other stanzas
in the poem have a richer mellowness, reveal a finer
sensitiveness than any in Collins's lovely *Ode*. For all
that the melody derives from Collins, we are borne away
from him to the neighbourhood of Keats's great poem.

But Collins had a classical, almost Miltonic, sense of form; what he lacked in the richness of direct perception he supplied by his careful concentration of emotional effect: so that, despite the more splendid beauty of the elements of Clare's poem, we dare not say it is really as fine as Collins's *Ode*. Collins gathers up all his more exiguous perceptions into a single stimulus to emotion: Clare lets them fall one by one, careless of his amazing jewels. Set his *Autumn* against Keats's three strophes, where the imagination has come to crystallize perceptions not less rich in themselves than Clare's into a single symbol—the very spirit of Autumn.

> Who hath not seen thee oft amid thy store?
>   Sometimes whoever seeks abroad may find
> Thee sitting careless on a granary floor
>   Thy hair soft lifted by the winnowing wind;
> Or on a half-reaped furrow sound asleep
>   Drowsed with the fume of poppies, while thy hook
> Spares the next swathe and all its twined flowers;
> And sometimes like a gleaner thou dost keep
>   Steady thy laden head across a brook
>   Or by a cyder-press, with patient look,
> Thou watchest the last oozings hours by hours.

Clare could not do that; for Keats had Collins's art and Clare's richness of perception, and he had also that incomparable imaginative power which alone can create the perfect symbol of an overwhelming and intricate emotion.

Yet we need to invoke Keats to explain Clare, and to understand fully why his wealth of perception was refined into so few perfect poems. Collins himself is not sufficient for the purpose; one cannot well invoke the success of a poorer to explain the failure of a richer nature. Keats, the great poetic artist, however, subsumes Clare. Careless critics, confusing the life of every day with the life of the poetic mind, rebuke Keats for his lack of discipline. Yet where in English poetry shall we find a power of poetic discipline greater than his, a more determined and inevitable compulsion of the whole of a poet's emotional experience into the single symbol, the one organic and inevitable form? In him were combined miraculously the humanity that can reject no element of true experience and the artistic integrity to which less than a complete mastery and transformation of experience is intolerable. When, therefore, we invoke Keats to explain Clare, when we feel the need to merge Clare into Keats in thought in order that we may discover his own poetic fulfilment, by completing the great pattern of which he is a fragment, we are passing a judgement upon the value and quality of Clare's own work of which the implications are unescapable. It is a fragment, but it is a fragment of the Parthenon pediment, of intrinsic value, unique, and beyond price.

Clare's qualities were authentic and without alloy. It was the power to refine and shape his metal that was denied him; his workshop is littered not with dross but with veritable gold—of melody, of an intensity of perception (truly, his 'mind was burned'), and, more rarely, of flashes of that passion of the pure imagination which is the mysterious source of the magic of poetry. Let our partial quotation of *Song's Eternity* suffice to prove the quality of his spontaneous melody. For the intensity of perception we may choose at random any page in this book. Is not a picture such as this cast upon 'that inward eye'?

> Where squats the hare to terrors wide awake
> Like some brown clod the harrows failed to break.

Such things are scattered throughout Clare; they range from the quiet vision of the actual, focused by a single word, such as

> The old pond with its water-weed
> And danger-daring willow tree,
> Who leans, an ancient invalid,
> O'er spots where deepest waters be,

to the authentic fancy of

> Here morning in the ploughman's songs is met
> Ere yet one footstep shows in all the sky,
> And twilight in the East, a doubt as yet,
> Shows not her sleeve of gray to know her by.

How perfect is the image, as perfect to its context and emotion as the 'sovran eye' of Shakespeare's sun! And what of the intense compression of a phrase like 'ploughed lands thin travelled by half-hungry sheep', precise not merely to a fact, but to an emotion?

This unmistakable core of pure emotion lies close to the surface throughout Clare. His precision is the precision of a lover; he watches nature as a man might watch his mistress's eyes; his breath is bated, and we seem to hear the very thumping of his heart; and there are moments when the emotion seems to rise in a sudden fountain and change the thing he sees into a jewel. 'Frail brother of the morn' to a jetty snail is the tender cry of a passionate lover; there is a delicateness in the emotion expressed which not even Wordsworth could attain when he called upon the Lesser Celandine. It is love of this kind that gives true significance to the poetry of nature, for only by its alchemy can the thing seen become the symbol of the thing felt: washed by the magic tide of an overwhelming emotion, the object shines with a pure and lucid radiance, transformed from a cause to a symbol of delight, and thus no longer delighting the senses and the emotions alone, but the mind. This mysterious faculty is not indeed the highest kind of poetic imagination, in which the intellect plays a greater part in the creation of the symbol; this emotional creation leaps from particular to particular, it lacks that endorsement from a centre of disciplined experience which is the mark of the poetic imagination at its highest: but it is purely poetic and truly creative.

In this authentic kind Clare was all but a master, and it may even be suspected that his unique gift would have suffered if he had possessed that element of technical control which would have made him a master indeed. For when we come to define as narrowly as we can the distinctive, compelling quality of his emotion, we find that in addition to tenderness we need the word impulsive. Clare's most beautiful poetry is a gesture of impulsive tenderness. It has a curious suddenness, almost a catch in the voice.

> The very darkness smiles to wear
> The stars that show us God is there.

We find, too, a still more authentic mark of the tenderness of impulsive love in his way of seeing his birds and beasts as ever so little absurd. 'Absurd' has a peculiar and delightful meaning in the converse of lovers; Clare's firetail is 'absurd' in precisely the same sense.

> Of everything that stirs she dreameth wrong,
> And pipes her 'tweet-tut' fears the whole day long.

And so, too, are his bees—the 'grandfather bee', the wild bees who 'with their legs stroke slumber from their eyes', 'the little bees with coal-black faces, gathering sweets from little flowers like stars'; even the riddle of the quail appears to be rather a delicate and lovable

waywardness in the bird than a mere ignorance in the
man.

> Among the stranger birds they feed,
>   Their summer flight is short and low;
> There's very few know where they breed
>   And scarcely any where they go.

A tenderness of this exquisite and impulsive kind might
have been damaged as much as strengthened by a firmer
technical control; a shiver of constraint might have
crept into the gesture itself and chilled it; and perhaps
we may touch the essential nature of Clare's emotion
most closely in the mysterious and haunting Asylum
poem, discovered by the present editors, and called by
them *Secret Love*.

> I hid my love when young till I
> Couldn't bear the buzzing of a fly;
> I hid my love to my despite
> Till I could not bear to look at light:
> I dare not gaze upon her face
> But left her memory in each place;
> Where'er I saw a wild flower lie
> I kissed and bade my love good-bye.
>
> I met her in the greenest dells
> Where dewdrops pearl the wood blue bells,
> The lost breeze kissed her bright blue eye,
> The bee kissed and went singing by;
> A sunbeam found a passage there,
> A gold chain round her neck so fair;
> As secret as the wild bee's song
> She lay there all the summer long.
>
> I hid my love in field and town
> Till e'en the breeze would knock me down,
> The bees seemed singing ballads o'er,
> The fly's bass turned a lion's roar;

And even silence found a tongue
To haunt me all the summer long;
The riddle nature could not prove
Was nothing else but secret love.

Clare is invoking the memory of Mary Joyce, the girl lover whom he did not marry, and who, though long since dead, lived for him as his true wife when he was immured in the asylum. But the fact of this strange passion is less remarkable than its precise quality; it is an intolerable tenderness, an unbearable surge of emotion eager to burst forth and lavish itself upon an object. Whether it was his passion for Mary Joyce which first awakened him to an awareness of the troublous depths of emotion within we cannot tell, for this poem is in itself no evidence of fact. But it bears witness unmistakable to the quality of the emotion which underlay all that is characteristic and unforgettable in his poetry.

When we have touched the unique emotional core which persists throughout the work of a true poet, we have come perhaps as near as we can to his secret. We stand as it were at the very source of his creation. In the great poetic artist we may follow out the intricacies and ramifications of the intellectual structure by which he makes the expression of his central emotion complete, and the emotion itself permanent. In Clare the work is unnecessary. The emotion is hardly mediated at all. The poetic creation is instinctive and impulsive; the love is poured out, and the bird, the beast, the flower is made glorious. It is the very process which Stendhal described, with fitting brilliancy, as *la cristallisation de l'amour*.

We may therefore most truly describe Clare as the love poet of nature; and we need not pause to explore the causes why nature and not a human being was turned to crystal by the magical process of his love. Those who care to know may find the story woven in among the narrative of Mr. Blunden's sympathetic introduction; they can discover for themselves the reason why Clare appears in the world of grown men and women as a stranger and a changeling; why the woman of his dreams is disembodied; why, when he calls to her in his *Invitation to Eternity*, the present is 'marred with reason'—

> The land of shadows wilt thou trace,
> Nor look nor know each other's face;
> The present marred with reason gone,
> And past and present both as one?
> Say, maiden, can thy life be led
> To join the living and the dead?
> Then trace thy footsteps on with me:
> We are wed to one eternity.

In eternity perhaps a woman, but in the actual Nature was Clare's mistress; her he served and cherished with a tenderness and faithful knowledge unique in the poetry of nature. Like a true lover he stammered in long speeches, but he spoke to her the divinest and most intimate things. Assuredly his lines were cast so that he had no need of woman even in eternity, and perhaps the truest words he ever wrote of himself are those of the poem by which he is most generally known:

> I long for scenes where man has never trod;
>   A place where woman never smiled nor wept;
> There to abide with my creator, God,
>   And sleep as I in childhood sweetly slept:
> Untroubling and untroubled where I lie;
>   The grass below—above the vaulted sky.

[JANUARY 1921.

VI

THE POETRY OF WALTER DE LA MARE

SINCE Plato turned his eyes, weary with the flux of things, to a celestial city whose aëry burgomasters kept guard over the perfect and unblemished exemplars of the objects of this bungled world, and a little while after, Jesus told his fishermen that they could find their peace only in the Kingdom of Heaven, where the mansions were innumerable, the subtle and the simple mind alike have been haunted by echoes of an unceasing music and dreams of imperishable beauty. Men's hearts have been swayed between a belief that the echoes and the dreams reached them from a distant eternal world more real than ours, and a premonition that the voice they heard was that of their own soul mysteriously calling them to self-perfection. And even those who have spoken with most conviction and persuasiveness, as though seeing face to face, of the perfect world immune from the rust of time have been the foremost to let fall the warning that their words were a parable. The rare spirits which steer the soul of humanity unite within themselves the contrary impulses of men. They live so intimately with their ideals that they are half persuaded of their reality; they think so highly of the soul that a truth for it alone becomes a truth. Therefore they can say in the same breath that the Father's house has many mansions and that the Kingdom of Heaven is within us, and no man can tell for certain whether *The Republic* is an allegory.

This dream or desire is one of the eternal themes of poetry, not because it is superficially more 'poetic' than any other, but because it contains one of the persistent realities of the soul. For if the soul lives in its own right, having a core of active being, it lives by an ideal. There is no escaping the fact of the Kingdom of Heaven which is within you, because it is the condition of the soul's vitality. Once begin to make choice between a worse and a better, and you are inevitably bound to recognize its validity; and to live without making the choice, whatever the intellect may tell us, is not life at all. Life, as we know it, cannot bar the gate against the ideal. If it is a dream, it is a dream we live by, and a dream we live by is more real than a reality we ignore.

But if this opposition of the ideal and the real is one of the great essential themes of poetry, it is also one which yields most to the impress of the poet's personality. Between the one pole of a complete belief in the existence of a kingdom of eternal beauty and imperishable perfection, and the other of an unfaltering recognition that these beatitudes exist in and for the soul alone, are infinite possibilities of faith and doubt, inexhaustible opportunities for the creative activity of art. For, apart from the precise mixture of certainty and hesitation in the poet's mind, one of the sovereign gestures of art is to make the ideal real, and to project a dim personal awareness on to a structure of definite inventions. The sense that we are exiled from our own country, that our rightful heritage has been usurped from us, we know not how, may impel one poet to create his kingdom in words and name it with names, people it with fit inhabitants, and another to record the bare fact of his consciousness as a homeless wanderer.

Mr. de la Mare is a poet of the great theme who is distinguished chiefly by his faculty of pressing invention and fancy to the service of his need. He has named his other kingdom with many names; it is Arabia,

Where the Princes ride at noon
'Mid the verdurous vales and thickets
Under the ghost of the moon.

It is Tartary; it is Alulvan. Queen Djenira reigns there,
and when she sleeps, she walks through

The courts of the lord Pthamasar,
Where the sweet birds of Psuthys are.

Or again it is Thule of the old legend, upon which the
poet beautifully calls:

If thou art sweet as they are sad
Who on the shore of Time's salt sea
Watch on the dim horizon fade
Ships bearing love and night to thee . . .

Within its shifting frontiers are comprised all the dim,
debatable lands that lie between the Never-Never
country of nursery rhyme and the more solid fields to
which the city mind turns for its paradise, the terrestrial
happiness which only a shake of the gods' dice-box has
denied:

Had the gods loved me I had lain
Where darnel is and thorn,
And the wild night-bird's nightlong strain
Trembles in boughs forlorn.

Nay, but they loved me not; and I
Must needs a stranger be
Whose every exiled day gone by
Aches with their memory.

That, surely, is a kingdom of solid earth. And yet we
wonder. Is it not also rather a symbol and projection
of the poet's desiderium, his longingness (to use his own

word), than an earthly kingdom from which fate has exiled him? We do not wonder long. The peace that comes from the satisfaction of this haunting desire is not to be found in any actual countryside. Nature has no medicinable balm for this unease. The poet himself tells us that he

> Oft marvelled who it was that sang
> Down the green valley languidly,
>   Where the grey elder thickets hang.
>
> Sometimes I thought it was a bird
>   My soul had charged with sorcery;
> Sometimes it seemed my own heart heard
>   Inland the sorrow of the sea.
>
> But even where the primrose sets
>   The seal of her pale loveliness,
> I found amid the violets
>   Tears of an antique bitterness.

Wherever the flux of things endures, this antique bitterness endures also. The loveliness of earth comes to the poet with the perpetual shadow of regret; and even the memory of it dissolves into nothingness:

> . . . Beauty vanishes; beauty passes;
>   However rare—rare it be;
> And when I crumble, who will remember
>   This lady of the West Country?

Life haunted by death, beauty by decay. What remedy will avail against this malady of mankind? Nothing but the courage of a dream. It is fitting, therefore, that the first, and presumably the earliest, of Mr. de la Mare's collected poems is an attempt to turn, as all the great idealists have tried to turn, the

ephemerality of earthly beauty into a proof of the existence of a beauty which endures for ever:

> The loveliest thing earth hath, a shadow hath,
> A dark and livelong hint of death,
> Haunting it ever till its last faint breath.
>   Who then may tell
> The beauty of heaven's shadowless asphodel?

But how to keep the courage of that dream—there is
the question. The poet belongs to the world of existence;
it is not possible for him to elude it. The shadowless
asphodel is haunted by the shadows of the earthly
flowers that have died. When the delight of fancy and
invention has begun to fade where shall the poet place
his other kingdom? What if Arabia and Tartary and
Thule and Alulvan cease to delight, and Queen Djenira
dream no more? Not all the princes of Arabia, with
their splendours and their music, can lull the poet's
mind into forgetfulness that he seeks not only a symbol,
but a satisfaction for his longing. There comes a time
when he knows that the delight of discovering a new
name is not the delight of discovered peace. The urgent,
incessant question begins to dominate, the pattern in
the carpet to appear.

The other kingdom is the kingdom of peace, the
country where the soul can rest. And now the poet no
more makes a triumphant deduction of immortality
from mortality, of the eternal from the temporal. He
declares his need, but the haven where it will be satisfied
is one which no earthly ship will find:

> Where blooms the flower when her petals fade,
> Where sleepeth echo by earth's music made,
> Where all things transient to changeless win,
> There waits the peace thy spirit dwelleth in.

And so, by nuances almost imperceptible of emotion and expression, we pass from this undiscoverable country to the clear, comfortless conclusion of what we must consider on this and on other grounds to be Mr. de la Mare's finest poem. In a sense *The Tryst* marks the end of his poetical journey. The curve is complete. The dream is only a dream.

> Think! in Time's smallest clock's minutest beat
> Might there not rest be found for wandering feet?
> Or 'twixt the sleep and wake of Helen's dream,
> Silence wherein to sing love's requiem? [1]
>
> No, no. Nor earth, nor air, nor fire, nor deep
> Could lull poor mortal longingness asleep.
> Somewhere there Nothing is; and there lost man
> Shall win what changeless vague of peace he can.

On the path of that curve all Mr. de la Mare's memorable poetic achievements—and they are many—will be found. On it, too, will be found the greater part of those rhymes for children which, to the casual glance, seem to be eccentric to it. For, as we have said, Arabia is on the same continent as the Never-Never land of the nursery rhyme; they march with one another. They were created to satisfy the same impulse. In the magic kingdom of childhood 'the shadowless asphodel' seemed really to exist, in a realm where all perfections and splendours and beauties persisted without change; and one might truly regard Mr. de la Mare's 'grown-up' poetry as an effort to recapture the simple certainty of that childhood belief, or to express the regret at the shadows that have encroached upon it. Therefore, his rhymes for children take a definite place in his poetry as a whole, and are also essentially different from other

[1] See note, p. 191.

rhymes of the kind; they are the natural, inevitable expression of the poet's deepest feeling. How natural and inevitable can be seen, if not from the tenor of this exposition, from the final verse of the exquisite poem, *Dreams*:

> What can a tired heart say,
> Which the wise of the world have made dumb?
> Save to the lonely dreams of a child,
>   'Return again, come!'

To recognize that the dream is a dream, yet to refuse to put it away, this is the vital act of comprehension which animates the enduring part of the poetry of the present age. It is a reflection of our devastating experience and our shadowy faith; for even while we know that the dream is a dream, having no counterpart in the reality without us, it cannot be wholly surrendered because we live by its enchantment. For to live is to make ourselves of a certain quality, to fashion ourselves to a certain temper; and if the dream is impotent to reshape the stubborn world beyond us, its power to work upon our own souls is undiminished.

When we say, therefore, that Mr. de la Mare's poetry is characteristic of the age, it is not in the sense that there is much poetry of the same quality to be found in our magazines and bookshops to-day—there is, alas, very little—but that it makes an appeal to, and in a way satisfies minds which have been tempered by the common experience. The strings have been so tightened that they respond to this touch. At a price we have purchased wisdom; clamour rings empty in our ears, we turn a mistrustful eye upon ambitious structures; superficialities—and these are commonest in the poetry of to-day—inspire in us an extreme repulsion. We respond only to the expression of the truth of our experience, and turn away from the pompous platitude and the laborious paradox which are generally offered to us as poetry.

In the vast wreckage of faiths with which the modern consciousness is strewn, there remains one thing in which we may believe without fear of disillusion; we may believe in beauty. We may even in the exaltation of despair, say with conviction that the wreckage of our hopes and the ruin of the world is beautiful. But the effort of contemplation so austere and self-regardless is too great to be maintained; we have not the strength to be Spinozas for more than a moment. And, even if we cannot make our beauty so all-inclusive we can still believe in the more partial and more human beauty we discern. But the condition of our belief is that we shall not deceive ourselves. Beauty is transient, we cannot by doting make it changeless. Where changeless beauty exists, there, indeed, our home may be; but we have only a dim memory of it to set against the certainty that the road leading back has been lost for ever.

Nevertheless, and in spite of the regret with which beauty must ever be attended, the faith in it endures; for the discernment of beauty is a mode of perception that is adequate to all the fates can bring. Disillusion has no power against it; it can not merely conquer, but make part of itself its regret for its own impotence. If it inspires men to build dream cities whose walls are proof against ephemeral corruption, it also inspires them to discover beauty in the recognition that their city is unsubstantial.

> And some win peace who spend
> The skill of words to sweeten despair
> Of finding consolation where
> Life has but one dark end;

Who, in rapt solitude, tell o'er
A tale as lovely as forlore,
Into the midnight air.

This winning of peace that haunts the mind of the poet is nothing other than communion with beauty. And if this beauty, which in spite of all can still be discerned and won, yields but a precarious peace, where the brave dream of youth promised one that would be secure, it could not well be otherwise, and the lovers of beauty are perhaps more fortunate than the lovers of justice, or of love.

In Mr. de la Mare's poetry we discover a trembling poise between the longing for an eternality of beauty and an acquiescence, an almost ecstatic acquiescence, in its transitoriness. Between those two conditions lies the gamut of emotional suggestion on which he plays with a consummate skill. They correspond to the deep, antithetical realities of the soul that have vexed men and poets and philosophers through the ages. The old debate between the One and Many is indeed changed, as it must be in the glancing mirror of an artist's mind. It is no longer a question which is true, but which the poet desires to be true. And can he tell? How shall he really choose between the static, eternal beauty whose ghost haunts the beauty that vanishes and passes, and the beauty which has sorrow 'more beautiful than beauty's self' to attend its passing?

The one whispers to the heart of the man; the other is a magnet to the soul of the artist. The beauty the poet perceives, the transitory gleam at which he snatches, cheats him with a mirage of unchanging perfection, of an imperishable beauty beyond the beautiful thing; yet the peculiar preciousness of the gleam he captures comes not least from its mortality. It is, indeed, more

beautiful because it is evanescent. No lasting comrade-
ship with happiness could bring half the enchantment
of the vision of

> Joy, whose hand is ever at his lips
> Bidding adieu.

And if poets have indulged the child and the man
within them with memories of the clouds of glory which
they trailed, and the thought that here they have no
abiding city, they have done it in part in order that
they may more exactly respond to the strange quality
of their true condition. If we can once persuade ourselves that we are princes of the blood-royal who wander
unknown in rags, how much keener grows our sense of
the infinite variety of life's vicissitude. It is, in short,
neither the ideal nor the real which fascinates the true
poet, but their incessant and conflicting interplay.
Each is a light which illuminates the other with 'an
unearthly gleam'; without the real to give it substance,
the dream is clear, calm, and colourless; without the
dream to give it shadow, the real is a vague and
confused chaos.

Beauty, which we may truly worship, is a jewel of
many facets. It gathers the radiance of the Many; it
diffuses the ray of the One. The poet seeks to borrow
both its powers, according to his mood; and we may
contrast and compare his moods, but to find them
contradictory is to make ourselves guilty of the old
crime of seeking logic where logic has no place. Mr. de la
Mare writes symbolically of the soul:

> Why did you flutter in vain hope, poor bird,
>   Hard-pressed in your small cage of clay?
> 'Twas but a sweet, false echo that you heard,
>   Caught only a feint of day.

Still is the night all dark, a homeless dark.
   Burn yet the unanswering stars. And silence brings
The same sea's desolate surge—sans bound nor mark—
   Of all your wanderings.

Fret now no more; be still. Those steadfast eyes,
   Those folded hands, they cannot set you free;
Only with beauty wake wild memories—
   Sorrow for where you are, for where you would be.

There beauty diffuses the radiance of the One, vexes
the soul with the memories of a lost perfection. Man,
like the Adam of another poem, 'still must roam a world
where sin and beauty whisper of home'. But in *Fare
Well*, which is the envoy to the collection called *Motley*,
beauty appears as the power which gathers the radiance
of the Many and brings to the soul the comfort of
a fleeting, but earthly, paradise:

   Look thy last on all things lovely
   Every hour. Let no night
   Seal thy sense in deathly slumber
      Till to delight
   Thou hast paid thy utmost blessing;
   Since that all things thou wouldst praise
   Beauty took from those who loved them
      In other days.

Yes, Mr. de la Mare belongs to the company which has
sought 'the principle of beauty in all things'. It is a quest
which, followed in singleness of heart, takes the great
poet into strange countries by strange roads. And if
Mr. de la Mare has not yet been led into the wilderness,
never stumbled across the temple floor to face the awful
question of Moneta, he has none the less given a perfect
expression to some of the deepest and most characteristic
moods of this generation.

                          [SEPTEMBER 1920.

VII

'ARABIA DESERTA'

IT is strangely and appropriately exhausting to read steadily through the two stout volumes of Doughty's *Arabia Deserta*. There are no suave and saving mists to mitigate our contact with that grim, basaltic waste, whose inhabitants seem to live in some close communion with the primeval rock of which their deserts were made. At most, to vary the deadly clarity of this 'seeing of a hungry man', we find traces of a fever passing over his vision, troubling it indeed, but troubling it only in such a way that it becomes for the moment superhumanly, menacingly clear—the reflection of a brightness through a burning crystal.

Travels in Arabia Deserta is a great book for the simplest and most sufficient of reasons: it is a direct enlargement of human experience. The burden of the new experience is at times all but intolerable. We are made to suffer torments of thirst, of hunger, of heat, of the fanatical cruelty of men. Nothing is interposed between our sensitiveness and the barren, yet austerely beautiful reality, and if there are moments when the strange reality is bathed in the quality of a dream, it is because the traveller's most enduring flesh and blood had reached the limit of its power. It is a dream to us because it was a dream to him.

Part of the fascination of the book lies, no doubt, in the indomitable courage of body and soul of the self-effacing man who hides behind it; but it is only because this twofold courage was transformed (yet without losing its peculiar and unfamiliar virtues) into a courage wholly of the world of art that we are able to surrender ourselves to the influence of the personality of which the book is so complete an expression. For *Arabia Deserta* is a triumph both of art and of personality. All great books are that, in some degree; yet the duality holds good of Mr. Doughty's masterpiece in a peculiar and perhaps unique sense: for Mr. Doughty is rather the writer of one great book than a great writer. He is a man who, whether by good fortune or careful choice, found the subject pre-eminently fitted to his character and his gifts; who realized his opportunity and his responsibility, and devoted himself entirely over a long space of years to the task of completely crystallizing his sensibility about the core of a subject which he recognized to be mysteriously congenial.

We feel, indeed, that no other theme could have called forth the whole of Mr. Doughty's powers. His poems, remarkable though they are, are fragmentary and uneven in comparison with *Arabia Deserta*; their pure and pellucid beauties are too often hidden away in the crannies of a complex structure and an obscure language which the author's imaginative power has not been sufficient to dominate or to fuse. Mr. Doughty's imaginative range is essentially narrow, and this very narrowness, which has made of his poems a comparative failure, has been one of the most potent elements in the triumphant achievement of *Arabia Deserta*. Here, in the attempt to record imperishably the lineaments of a secret and inhospitable land and of the people it has produced to be its denizens, was no need of that elasticity of the imagination which is necessary to great poetry. The needs were opposite to this: first, of that amazing courage of body and spirit which enabled him to wander unfriended for two years among nomad tribesmen, in whom the traditional hospitality fought ever a doubtful

battle with their hatred of the Christian, and whose
living (even when they were friendliest) was of a harsh-
ness and scarcity hardly imaginable to the European;
then, in order to understand and sympathize with them,
of a measure of that religious sternness which daily
threatened him; and, last and greatest, of the patience
to hammer out of the English speech a language apt to
render this strange, ageless Semitic world, where the
shadows of mind and earth are black and the lights
glaring, where there is neither haze nor hesitation, and
the thoughts of three thousand years of Western civilization are utterly unknown.

From what we have called, somewhat roughly and
ungraciously, Mr. Doughty's narrowness all these needs
could be supplied. His own disposition was towards
spiritual issues made, to a modern sense, inhumanly
clear. Against fanaticism he could pit a stubbornness
which itself seems little short of the fanatical; to strike
against the religious rock of the Arabs he found steel in
himself.

'And as we drank around they bade me call myself a
"Misslim", and in my heart be still of what opinion I would
(this indulgence is permitted in the koran to any persecuted
Moslemin)—words not far from wisdom; and I have often
felt the iniquitous fortune of travelling thus, an outlawed
man (and in their sight worthy of death), only for a name,
in Arabia. It had cost me little or naught to confess Kon-
fuchu or Socrates to be apostles of Ullah; but I could not
find it in my life to confess their barbaric prophet of Mecca,
and enter, under the yoke, their solemn fools' paradise.'

Indeed, the elements of a martyr were in Mr. Doughty,
and many were the times towards the end of his pil-
grimage when he came within a hairsbreadth of what
had been martyrdom of the purest kind; and the very

straitness of his detestation of Islam brought him nearer than any politic complaisance could have done to an understanding of those for whom Mohammed is truly the prophet of God. Again in his predilections in the English language itself Mr. Doughty knows no compromise; he is, one might fairly say, an Old Believer; Spenser first, and Chaucer second, are his gods, and there is none beside them. For him the magnificent efflorescence of the language of Shakespeare and Milton might never have been; hardly even the English Bible.

Such then was the man who measured himself with unknown Arabia—a man of a higher and more enlightened tradition, but of a similar basic austerity. No man more proof against the assaults of Arabia ever entered into her; and none more fitted by temper, or by experiences to be endured by that temper alone, to be her patient recreator. None ever compromised less with the Arabs; none was ever more respected by them. If we have regard, therefore, either to the quality of the achievement in *Arabia Deserta* or to the evident character of the man who wrote it, we are not surprised that ten years went to its composition. It is, as it were, hewn painfully out of the rock or hammered out of stubborn iron; never, even when Mr. Doughty handles his language with the most assured mastery, does an all but imperceptible sense of strain depart from it, and the ensuing tension is essential to the story he has to tell, the emotion he has to convey. An effort is demanded of the reader which corresponds (in another kingdom) to the effort demanded of Mr. Doughty; an effort richly rewarded, as was his own. No slovenly attention will suffice to receive the message of this marvellous description of a summer day in the Arabian desert:

'Now longwhile our black booths had been built upon the sandy stretches, lying before the swelling white Nefud side: the lofty coast of Irnan in front, whose cragged breaches, where is any footing for small herbs nourished of this barren atmosphere, are the harbour of wild goats, which never drink. The summer's night at end, the sun stands up as a crown of hostile flames from that huge covert of inhospitable sandstone bergs; the desert day dawns not little and little, but it is noontide in an hour. The sun, entering as a tyrant upon the waste landscape, darts upon us a torment of fiery beams, not to be remitted till the far-off evening.—No matins here of birds; not a rock partridge-cock, calling with blithsome chuckle over the extreme waterless desolation. Grave is that giddy heat upon the crown of the head; the ears tingle with a flickering shrillness, a subtle crepitation it seems, in the glassiness of this sun-stricken nature: the hot sand-blink is in the eyes, and there is little refreshment to find in the tent's shelter; the worsted booths leak to this fiery rain of sunny light. Mountains looming like dry bones through the thin air, stand far around about us: the savage flank of Ybba Moghrair, the high spire and ruinous stacks of el-Jebal, Chebad, the coast of Helwan! Herds of weak nomad camels waver dispersedly, seeking pasture in the midst of this hollow, fainting country, where but lately the swarming locusts have fretted every green thing. This silent air burning about us, we endure breathless till the *assr*: when the dazing Arabs in the tents revive after their heavy hours. The lingering day draws down to the sun-setting; the herds-men, weary of the sun, come again with the cattle, to taste in their menzils the first sweetness of mirth and repose.— The day is done, and there rises the nightly freshness of the purest mountain air: and then to the cheerful song and the cup at the common fire. The moon rises ruddy from that solemn obscurity of Jebal like a mighty beacon:—and the morrow will be as this day, days deadly drowned in the sun of the summer wilderness.'

This is the achievement of a pure and deliberate

art; very little prose of this assured magnificence has
been written in our day; and certainly no other book
has been maintained on such a level for centuries.
Arabia Deserta is incomparable.

If we are required to furnish a phrase to describe its
unique quality, we should say that it was distinguished
above all by a hard, ascetic purity. We are conscious
from the opening sentence that we are taken apart into
a world of thought and living remote from our own,
a world where man has shed many of the encumbrances
that muffle his contact with elemental things, and many
of the subtleties which seem to us inseparable from a
humane life—a world part parable, part fairy tale;
simpler yet sterner, more beautiful yet more oppressive
than our own; austerely intoxicating. The first draught
is overpowering.

'A new voice hailed me of an old friend when first
returned from the Peninsula, I paced along the
street of Damascus which is called Straight; and
suddenly taking me wondering by the hand, "Tell
me" (said he), "since thou art here again in the peace
and assurance of Ullah, and whilst we walk, as in the
former years, toward the new blossoming orchards, full
of the sweet spring as the garden of God, what moved
thee, or how couldst thou take such journeys into the
fanatic Arabia?"'

From this, the first sentence of the book, we are lost,
as though lifted on a magic carpet out of time, to wander
in an ecstasy of desolation through regions which have
not changed since the world began, to consort with
Abraham and the sons of Abraham as they were, but
for their coffee and their guns, infinite ages ago. No
wonder then that even to the traveller himself, as the

pangs of hunger lightened the ballast of his brain, the life became as a timeless dream.

'Hither lies no way from the city of the world, a thousand years pass as one daylight; we are in the world and not in the world, where Nature brought forth man, an enigma to himself, and an evil spirit sowed in him the seeds of dissolution. And looking then upon that infinite spectacle, this life of the wasted flesh seemed to me ebbing, and the spirit to waver her eyas wings unto that divine obscurity.'

Yet this is a dream where things become not soft and vaporous but of an awful solidity: the vast volcanic table-lands of basalt rock, jutting through the kinder sand, are not more gaunt than the fanatic hatred of the Moslem for the Nasrany that looms always behind even the most ceremonious hospitality of the tents. It would have been less than human if the wanderer's spirit had never come near to failing, and he had never asked in despair: 'Wherefore should I macerate my life continually in the greatest jeopardy? Or suffer this distress of soul, to kick against the fanaticism of the whole Ishmaelite country?'

Behind, incessantly lifting and maintaining the book, is the man. The singular unity of the artist and the man makes it impossible for us to regard the book for long merely as one of the finest examples of English artificial prose. It is that indeed, and we have to keep this aspect before our eyes in order rightly to appreciate his solitary and so long neglected achievement. But the garment of his style fits the man so closely that unless we diligently remember the ten years' labour we may lapse back into thinking that the writing was natural in the common sense of the word. Because we can see that only Mr. Doughty could have forged and manipulated this language, we may persuade ourselves that the work was easy, though in fact nothing is harder in literature than to impress upon our minds the sense of a strong and coherent personality.

Nevertheless, though *Arabia Deserta* must in the last resort be judged as a work of deliberate art, and though it will stand for many years on the rock of this rare excellence, there is a danger of neglecting its simpler virtues as a story of adventure. It is not possible to regard the thrilling sequence of ever more desperate encounters at Hayil, at Kheybar, at Aneyza, and the final jeopardy outside Mecca when even the hidden pistol, Doughty's last resource, was torn away, and the sudden drop into the final calm of the Sherif's kindly reception at Tayif, as ordered by a sense of artistic culmination. Mr. Doughty, we feel, sticks close to the facts. But the collaboration of events toward the single effect is almost bewildering. We are borne irresistibly along to the utmost limits of one man's endurance. The traveller, we feel as we follow him on the last journey from Aneyza to the confines of Mecca, must be saved or he will die, if not by the sword of the ruffian Salem, from the sheer weakness of a broken man. It has been too much; we are oppressed and weary with the horror of the unequal struggle.

To read *Arabia Deserta* is to live out a whole life in the Arabian waste, and to reach the end fordone. The interludes of peace in the nomad tents and of bountiful beauty in the oases were too few to give the traveller back his strength; at each stage some vital force had ebbed that could not be restored. But the beauty of these resting-places appears to us in the barren meagreness about as a celestial enchantment.

'Oh, what bliss to the thirsty soul is in that light, sweet water, welling soft and warm as milk from the rock! And

I heard the subtle harmony of Nature, which the profane cannot hear, in that happy stillness and solitude. Small, bright dragon-flies, azure, dun, and vermilion, sported over the cistern water ruffled by a morning breath from the figgera, and hemmed in the solemn lava-rock. The silver fishes glance beneath, and white shells lie at the bottom of this water world. I have watched there the young of the thob shining like scaly glass and speckled: this fairest of saurians lay sunning, at the brink, upon a stone; and oft-times moving upon them and shooting out the tongue, he snatched his prey of flies without ever missing.—Glad were we when Jummar had filled our girby of this sweet water.'

With a like more than human sweetness amid the fierce fanaticism appears the kindness of the few who succoured him, the Arab women in the tents, El-Kenneyny at Aneyza, Amm Mohammed at Kheybar, from whom this was the leave-taking:

' "Now God be with thee, my father Mohammed, and requite thee."—"God speed thee, Khalil," and he took my hand. Amm Mohammed went back to his own, we passed further; and the world, and death, and the inhumanity of religions parted us for ever.'

The kindly men and women and the few hours of rest shine out like jewels from this narrative, which, we know even without Colonel Lawrence's authoritative word to confirm it, holds within it all the sights and sounds, the spirit and the people of Arabia, 'smelling of *samn* and camels'. And something, at least, of their power to outlast centuries has entered into it; for it is a book built solidly, and not as books are built to-day. Therefore it has been slow in coming to its own. It is more than thirty years since the first edition was published; and now we have only reached the third. In 1888 Mr. Doughty wrote in his preface: 'We set but

but over the austere rhythm of the final sentence hovers
the memory of more opulent sonorities:

'Grave is that giddy heat upon the crown of the head; the
ears tingle with a flickering shrillness, a subtle crepitation it
seems, in the glassiness of this sun-stricken nature: the hot
sand-blink is in the eyes, and there is little refreshment to
find in the tents' shelter; the worsted booths leak to this fiery
rain of sunny light.

Nearly fifty years lay between those two memories. The
Doughty who wrote *Arabia Deserta* was a young man—
the book over which he laboured so many years was
published before he was forty; the Doughty who
returned to literature in 1906 with an epic poem was
an old one.

But the difference between those two memories is not
at all the difference between prime and decline: there
is a change, but not towards decrepitude. The touch
is firm, and the hand full of cunning in the later picture
as in the earlier; what has intervened is a change, or
a sublimation, of temper. The strange immediacy of
sensation which makes *Arabia Deserta* so overpowering
has given way to a spiritual remoteness. The same
things are remembered, yet how differently! Between
Arabia Deserta and Doughty's subsequent writing there
is a division which is almost a gulf. Though there were
twenty-five years between *Arabia Deserta* and *The Dawn
in Britain*, it is not a temporal division; though *Arabia
Deserta* is prose and the rest of Doughty's writing poetry,
it is not a division of literary kinds; it is a spiritual
metamorphosis. In fact it must have been gradual; but
in the long silence of twenty-five years there is nothing
to prepare us, nothing to mediate by gentle transitions
the sudden shock of his uncouth epic.

And, when we have meditated upon it, we begin to see how fortunate was the accident which gave us *Arabia Deserta*. In the nomad life of the inhospitable desert Doughty had found, by a premonitory instinct, the only human society he could accept. When he went to the Arab peninsula he was driven, scarce consciously, by the impulse to struggle his way backward through time away from the works of modern man; and he all but died in the effort. Why, we ask ourselves again and again, as we read his story, does he stay? Why does not he escape? The inscriptions that were his nominal excuse meant little or nothing to him; there was no thought of profit, none even of 'experience'. He was there, he knew not why nor how; for the cause lay deeper than his consciousness. If he was to live active in the world of men, it was among such men that he must live, men who believed fiercely and loved and hated simply—men who were truly of one substance with the earth wherein they lived. He stayed among them to the moment when, if he stayed longer, he would have died, because it was a real world to him: in it he *lived*. In it were men and women he understood and who understood him, and his pictures of them have a direct Homeric truth. In the pages of *Arabia Deserta* the society of men among whom he could *live* lives again. When that book was finished Doughty's work was over: he had done perfectly what no other man could have done at all; he had carved an enduring image of a simple Semitic people whose hate was more real to him than a European's love.

After many years *The Dawn in Britain* appeared. It was an epic on the grand pattern in twenty-four books, telling of men and gods and godlike men. But Doughty had already written his epic. The Aarab and Beduwy

with whom he had lived were real men; he had had but
to describe them as he had known them. Not so with
his primitive Britons, who were the work of his imagination. His Arabs live, his Celts do not. *Arabia Deserta* has
the actuality of Homer; *The Dawn in Britain* is, after all,
wholly artificial. So, one might say, is the *Aeneid*. But,
first, the world of Aeneas was by no means so remote
from Virgil as that of Caractacus from Doughty; second,
Virgil used his story as the means by which every tremor
of a subtle consciousness might find expression; and,
third, he was creating at once a new poetry and a new
language. So Doughty himself in *Arabia Deserta* had
struck new fires out of the English speech; he is fanatical,
but not in his language. In *The Dawn in Britain* his
fanaticism has invaded his art.

Whatever the language of *Arabia Deserta* may be, it is
not primitive: it has the richness of a fine eclecticism
and a sure sense of propriety. To secure his effects
Doughty freely chose the finest tools. But by the time
he had begun to write poetry he had become possessed
by a theory of diction, derived not from any considera-
tion of the language itself, but wholly from moral pre-
possessions. In Spenser, he held, English had reached
its brief perfection, and in him already had begun to
decline. Chaucer he could with an effort accept, but he
could never mention him without heaving a sigh over
the broadness of Geoffrey's humour. But with these two
men the English language began and ended for Doughty
the poet. Such a phrase as 'a subtle crepitation' became
impossible to him.

There may seem to have been a certain wisdom in his
deliberate archaism. He had determined to write of
early Britons: then why not use the English language
when it is nearest to their simplicity, yet still an English

language? Perhaps it was with some such argument
that Doughty first persuaded himself; but it is an argument which forgot that when Spenser himself was
writing he was using all the resources of language as
freely as Doughty himself had done in his prose. A poet
cannot deny himself this freedom if his imaginations are
to be made real. But, in Doughty, the distinction
between asceticism of spirit and self-denial in the use
of language seems to have been obliterated; moreover,
he had come to regard himself as a man with a mission,
to restore to a degenerate nation the virtues and the
speech of olden time.

Doughty's poetry, in conception and in diction, is the
poetry of a fanatic; the spirit, which had served him so
well by steeling him to endure extreme hardship in the
desert at nature's hands and men's, now hardened
within him. In Arabia, and in writing of it, he had
expanded; now he contracted. There is in all his poetry
an intense patriotism, but it is a patriotism which loves
an ideal England and abhors the actual; the bitterness in
his denunciations of the democratic polity is vitriolic,
and it has a defect graver than its mere excess; it is
repellent even to those who might share his aversion
because it shows clearly that, if Doughty could have had
his way, he would have replaced democracy by something worse—a rigid and tyrannous theocracy. For in
his imagination God and England were one, precisely
as God and Israel were one to the Jews of old; and in
The Cliffs (1909) he pushes his idea relentlessly to the
point of savagery. In that poem the image of 'Sancta
Britannia' is precisely as the idol of a savage tribe; with
the decay of the warrior spirit it languishes, with the
revival under stress of invasion of the berserk mood it
regains power; but even at the last the image remains

blindfold. The veil can be removed from its eyes only by the hands of the only child of a young widow, and the child must die the moment its fingers touch the veil. And the child is sacrificed accordingly, as Mesha, King of Moab, slew his eldest son. Doughty had come to be unconscious of the distinction between patriotism and Moloch worship; and, more strangely still, he makes the horrible imagination worse by putting forward a chorus of elves who promise to the mother, while she holds the murdered baby in her arms,

> She widow shall not want, whilst elves can work:
> We would we might, in honey of wild bees,
> Embalm her blossom babe; whose little mound
> Will elves each summer night bestrew with flowers . . .

The man who could make fairies condone that inhuman sacrifice had become estranged from the spirit of the country he loved: his zeal had eaten him up.

To the rigour and perversity of his mind inevitably corresponded a rigour and perversity in his use of language: he became not merely archaistic, but insensitive and tyrannous. With a kind of frenzied implacability he would torture English syntax and compel words to do his bidding. Scarcely can a page be found of his poetry without lines of this kind:

> No more I knew: under a flag of truce
> Gathered at day the fallen were; and when us
> The surgeons had inspected one by one;
> I on the dead-cart was 'mongst soldiers dead
> Laid; and that driven then to the grave-trench was.
> There on the brinks those, shrouded in their cloaks
> White with night-rime, were in long rows, outlaied.

It is no use mincing words: that is something worse than idiosyncrasy; and it is never far away in Doughty's poetry. Sometimes the effect, if we can regard it in complete detachment, is comic (. . . burst were the water and gas Mains): but for the most part the manner is too much of a piece with the matter to permit such facile relief. Doughty is terribly humourless—it is never easy to laugh at a man whom one can never laugh with.

No criticism of his work would be adequate which did not insist that his poetry, in content and form alike, is of a lower order than *Arabia Deserta*: from beginning to end, save for one remarkable exception, it is warped. It is the poetry of a sectary, of a man of intense and narrow genius, who had once, and once for all, breathed a full breath among his semblables. The life that he had lived he rendered again: he lavished himself on the one human reality he had loved. The completeness of *Arabia Deserta* is narrow; but it is an absolute completeness; within those amazing pages is a universe, simple, primeval, but one where men are born and have their being and are gathered to their fathers. And Doughty's one great poem sprang directly from his experience of that eternal world. *Adam Cast Forth* is in essence a sublime simplification of all that he lived and learned in the Arabian desert. There he had become as the first man; under that implacable sun he had been as it were dissolved away into an elemental essence of mortality, he had become the I AM of man, the plaything yet the equal of his own ineffable but jealous God. If the pure sublime has ever been achieved in English poetry it is achieved in *Adam Cast Forth*: for in it man and God become almost indistinguishable in majesty, yet not, as in Milton, with a diminution of God. Man the creature is lifted up to his Creator. Again and again Doughty challenges Milton, and comes away, if not victorious,

completely without scathe. Milton's glory of language
is counterpoised by Doughty's intensity of realization.
When Adam tells the story of the Fall, and says simply:
'Then God was weary of us', the effect is overpowering:
one feels that in those six words is somehow crammed
a vision of the whole of human destiny. And Doughty
can meet Milton at the very pinnacle of his own perfection: he dares to rewrite Eve's encounter with her
own mirrored image. Here is the Milton:

> I thither went
> With unexperienced thought, and laid me down
> On the green bank, to look into the clear
> Smooth lake, that to me seemed another sky.
> As I bent down to look, just opposite
> A shape within the wat'ry gleam appeared,
> Bending to look upon me. I started back;
> It started back: but pleased I soon returned;
> Pleased it return'd as soon with answering looks
> Of sympathy and love; there had I fix'd
> Mine eyes till now, and pined with vain desire
> Had not a voice thus warned me. What thou seest,
> What there thou seest, fair Creature, is thyself.

All the resources of Milton's art are in motion there.
What can Doughty do against it? This is what he does:

> Therein I saw then, like an heavenly vision,
> Some Being more even than art thou O Adamu fair!
> The appearance of an Angel, that I knew not:
> Which, whilst I looked, seemed woman. I outstretched
> Mine hand: she likewise hand put forth toward mine.
>   Down, at the water's brink, to view more near
> This thing, I kneeled: she kneeled! I gazed upon her
> I laughed, I spake: she laughed then, but not spake.
> And in her other hand were fruits as these,
> And flowers like to mine. Surprised mine heart,

> I startling leapt; and plashed therein my foot.
>   Marred then the image was: she fled, alas!
> I saw her not again; though I descended
> To seek her, in the pool.

There is not in this the opulent, sensuous loveliness of the Milton; the rhythm, as ever in Doughty, is harsher and more abrupt: and yet Doughty exists, even beside Milton, sovereign in his own right. Doughty's Adama is not the equal of Milton's Eve, of course; but neither is Milton's Adam the equal of Doughty's Adamu.

Let us leave the swaying issue, remembering that *Adam Cast Forth* is not Doughty's epic poem. Would it had been! It is simply a poem of a little over a hundred pages, intense and sublime, written out of the knowledge of one who had been driven from oasis into desert and stumbled back to an earthly Eden again. Was it, we wonder, simply because Milton had preceded him, that Doughty sought his subject in ancient Britain? If it was, we have lost a masterpiece through a misconception; what Adamu might have been Milton did not know, and Doughty did. But he turned aside and plunged into the misty beginnings of these islands—a long, vague, intricate story which he, who had little or no architectonic gift, could not control. As we wander through its tortuous passages we have frequent glimpses of loveliness and grandeur: loveliness as in the tale of Crispin and Ogygia in Book I, or of Elsa and Cloten in Book III, or the fleeting pictures of England's graciousness which are given only to be snatched away, as this of the arrival of the Christians in England:

> Behold new birth of the long dying night,
> How day, with cheerful face, is springing wide!
> Sounds, of small fowl, the mingled sweet consent
> From river-brinks, of Britain's underwoods,

Warbling God's love, among their leafy bowers.
On trembling, lightsome, wings blithe lav'rock mounts.
With *iss-iss*! shrill, sheen swallows flit aloft;
And chants, from thicket-grove, lone nightingale.
And golden bees borne-by, on dawn's sweet breath,
To dewy hills. Hark cushots, sobbing soft.
Like unto bride seems this fair land adorned.

Within the ruggedness of their surroundings such lines
as these seem soft and gentle; but they also have in them
an unrelenting rigour, a rhythmical austerity that
reminds us that even the fairies of this poet's imagination smile upon blood-sacrifice. Yet Doughty was fond
of fairies: they appear in both *The Cliffs* and *The Clouds*;
but they are the fairies not of the delighted fancy, but
of some queer theology, sisters to daemons, daughters
of principalities and powers, unbending ministers of
Doughty's grim tribal god. We are told they dance,
we never feel they dance; we are told they sing, we never
hear them singing. These are a new kind of fairies in
whom one must believe on pain of excommunication,
or worse, who would not pinch us black and blue, but
torture us with red-hot pincers.

Doughty's real poetic splendours are not to be found in
such passages as these, not even in a passage of loveliness
so sustained as the Muses' garden with which *The Clouds*
opens; they are grim and grey, and pass almost unper-
ceived, yet they shine with a strange solemnity, like the
dark glint on steel. Such is this description of the morning after a storm on the Christians' voyage to England:

Though long be, till crude winter season change,
Dear to the saints, are their seafaring days;
Wherein new birth and childhood of their lives.
Fair is that fleeting fullness of the seas,
In whose round molten bosom their keel rides.

I

Falls now the storm, and sleep grey dapple waves:
Or these like fallows, and much furrowed field.
Whose springing blade is wallowed of the wind.
And aye sea's infinite bruit is in their ears,
Like to an everlasting voice of God. . . .

In still grimmer vein is this brief glimpse of the Pillars
of Hercules:

They see, where their keel fleets, thick bedded ribs;
(Clothed with long tangle-locks, of wild sea-wrack,
And shells,) of many drowned and broken ships:
And under rumbling caves strewed the white sand,
With skulls and dreary bones of mariners;
That to and fro, washed in cold-sliding billows,
Do make their everlasting moan, to God.

Such sudden things as these, and they are many, are
high poetry indeed. But Doughty, who could never
have become a little poet, lacked two things necessary
to the great one: comprehensiveness of mind and a
receptive sensibility. We feel that, after his great book,
he ceased to experience; he had taken one long gulp
at the cup of life that was offered him in his youth and
drained it to the lees. It was never refilled for him, or
if it was he put it away from him like a desert anchorite.
What he had known and suffered was life to him, and
there was no other. The primeval struggle of man
against the elements—this was real and true: the rest
of life was an ugly and evil dream. He set his face and
shut his heart against it. There is something magnificent
in the indomitable spirit of this lonely hero who, like
Ajax in the Underworld, stalks away and will not speak;
and his unbending spirit is in the steely monotony of
his verse. Doughty had received his revelation, once
for all, in the Arabian desert: to it nothing might be
added, from it nothing taken away.

BAUDELAIRE

PERHAPS no word has been more prolific of literary misunderstandings in the last half-century than the word decadence. Critics with the best will in the world, which is the will for exact description, have called writers decadent. The unfortunate writer has been damned by a definition that no one had troubled to understand. In the general mind to be decadent is to be impure, immoral, or, in the now more frequent and really more damaging phrase, to be 'unhealthy'. Many poets were branded as decadents in the nineteenth century. All of them suffered by the name; some deserved to suffer, and some did not. Charles Baudelaire, who was the first and greatest of the line, suffered most and deserved it least. He suffers still, because every critic who is convinced of his high excellence as a poet and is anxious to elucidate it is driven to dwell on the element of decadence in the man· and his work. The word is as necessary to the understanding of Baudelaire as a particular instrument to a surgeon for a particular operation.

Decadence is essentially a word of the historian who applies it to those periods in the history of a society when its old institutions are breaking down and being obscurely replaced by new; to ages when the transition is being made from one social ideal, one social fabric, to another. The word can be applied to literature, or art in general, in one of two ways. It can be used historically to distinguish the literature that is created during an age of decadence, or it can be used metaphorically to describe the literature of a period of transition between two literary ideals. These meanings are utterly different, yet the word is generally made to carry them both at the same time, as though a literary decadence were the necessary concomitant of a social decadence. Worse still, to the vagueness created by the fusion of these two meanings has been added a misty rec ction of orgies under the Roman Empire. A tinc-tu of fiddling Nero, Caligula, and Elagabalus gives a piquant flavour to the bolus of haziness. Writers and artists are called 'decadent' by people who mean that they are merely bad artists, or artists who deal with 'unhealthy' subjects. Thus a valuable word is ruined because it is used to save people the trouble of thinking.

It may be true, though it remains to be proved, that the literatures of all periods of decadence have certain elements in common; it is certainly untrue that the literature of such a period is necessarily inferior as literature (indeed Nietzsche argued, very plausibly, that the veritable heights of literature can be attained only in an age of decadence). In the case of Baudelaire it is extremely necessary that we should be clear in what sense the epithet decadent is used when it is applied to him. Baudelaire is the poet of an historical decadence; he is not in any useful sense of the word a decadent poet. On the contrary, he was one of the greatest and most assured poets that France has produced. As a poet, he was strong, masculine, deliberate, classical; not a puny successor of great men, but the heroic founder of a line; and the peculiar quality of his work derives from the interaction of these two very different factors, the decadence of the age in which he lived and his own poetic strength and determination. Not that his choice of subject may not sometimes be called perverse; but the perversity of his work is the least important, the least

relevant, and, to the unbiased reader, the least notice-
able of its qualities. It is easy for any poetaster to be
perverse; it is extremely difficult for a poet to be perverse
in Baudelaire's way. For Baudelaire was not a furtive
dabbler in unclean things; he was the deliberate and
determined poet of an attitude to life to which we cannot
refuse the epithet heroic. The driving impulse of his
work was not a predilection, but a conviction.

Baudelaire was convinced that the age in which he
lived was a decadence, and we who know it not only
by his own passionate protest against it, but by Balzac's
romantic anatomy of its corruption, must acquiesce in
his conviction. The old aristocratic order had fallen;
there was no new democratic order to supply its place :
in the interval arose, like a growth of weeds on the site
of a demolished building, as the sole principle of spiritual
and social order, that reverence for wealth for its own
sake which distinguished nineteenth-century France.
Guizot's *Enrichissez-vous* marked a social nadir. It was
the age of rampant industrialism and violent and
abortive revolution; of the hideous and uncontrolled
eruption of the great cities; of all the squalor of a
victorious and hypocritical materialism. Against this
tyranny Baudelaire conceived it his duty to protest,
not merely by the poetic utterance of cries of revolt but
by the actual conduct of his life. The French romantic
movement as a whole was animated to some extent by
a spirit of protest against the sordidness of the age; but
Baudelaire belonged to a curious section of the movement which had very little in common with romanticism
as we generally conceive it now. His affinities were
with the disciplined and contemptuous romanticism of
Stendhal and Mérimée. This romanticism was rather
a kind of sublimated realism, based upon an almost

morbid *horreur d'être dupe*—romantic in its aspiration away from the *bourgeois* society which it loathed, realistic in its determination to accept the facts as they were. It was romantic also in its conception and elaboration of the attitude which it considered inevitable for the chosen spirits who would not bow the knee to Baal.

It is important to grasp these two intimately woven strands of realism and romanticism in Baudelaire and his two predecessors. This strange but natural combination plays a great part not in the literature of France only, but in that of Europe as a whole during the last century. A single thread runs through the work of Stendhal, Mérimée, Baudelaire, Nietzsche, and Dostoevsky; in spite of their outward dissimilarity, and the great differences between their powers, these men are united by a common philosophical element which takes bodily shape in their conceptions of the hero. They are all intellectual romantics, in rebellion against life, and they imagine for themselves a hero in whom their defiance should be manifested. The three Frenchmen had in common, and put into actual practice, the ideal of 'le Dandy'. 'Le Dandy' is an imperturbable being above the law, inscrutable, contemptuous of the world, silent under the torments which it inflicts upon his sensitive soul, continually experimenting at his own risk with morality, exercising a drastic discipline upon himself, and adopting, as a symbol of his inward discipline, that elegance of outward appearance which we generally associate with the word 'dandy'. On the one side the conception of the Dandy touches the romantic literary ideal of the poet in his *tour d'ivoire*, on the other it reaches out in anticipation towards the superman of Nietzsche and the still subtler and more impressive antinomian hero of Dostoevsky's novels. In both these forms it

influenced Baudelaire's life as a man and activity as
a poet.

From this angle it is perhaps easier to understand and
analyse the almost massive impression of unity we receive
from so small a work as Baudelaire's. A volume of
poetry, a volume of prose (of which fully one-third is
a paraphrase of De Quincey's *Opium Eater*), two volumes
of scattered criticism, chiefly of painting, three volumes
of translations from Poe—these are the complete works
of Baudelaire. What is really original in them could
easily be contained in three pocket volumes. Yet the
abiding impression made by them is one of solidity.
This is in the main because the inspiration is single and
the foundations firm and invariable. As an artist
Baudelaire works from a single centre; his attitude to
life and his attitude to art lend each other aid and
confirmation. Even his vices as a poet have the merit
of being deliberate, and of contributing to the total
effect at which he aimed. They are the vices proper,
one might almost say essential, to his achievement.
When Baudelaire is rhetorical, his rhetoric is never
entirely empty; it has a dramatic propriety and significance in the mouth of the *âme damnée*, the rebellious
angel hurling defiance at the powers of heaven. When
he indulges his desire to astonish, he is asserting his
immunity from conventional fears. Both these vices,
it is true, betray in Baudelaire's mind some confusion
between the laws of heroism in life and in art. They are
not the less vices because they are intelligible. Nevertheless, it does make a difference that they are not
irrelevant. A writer's weaknesses are to some extent
condoned when they are seen to be the condition of his
strength.

It is Baudelaire's chief distinction that, in spite of

these one or two failures, he made a successful and undeviating effort to translate his ethical attitude towards life into a purely poetical gesture. He might so easily have been a poet of the confessional, pouring out his wounded soul in lyrical *cris de cœur*; but his 'Dandyism' helped him to a more truly poetic conception of his task. The fox might be tearing at his vitals, but there must be, if not a smile, an inscrutable expression of Spartan impassivity on his face. The self-sacrifice demanded of him by his moral creed coincided with the self-sacrifice demanded of him as a poet. That the original impulse was partly moral discounted nothing of his achievement, for he was in the fortunate position of one whose effort in life seconded his endeavours in art; and if he more often formulated his purpose in ethical terms, it was more because he was enough of a romantic to prefer the hero of life to the hero of art than because he was unable to envisage it as a poetic problem alone.

'Bien d'autres que moi' (he writes in *L'Art Romantique*), 'ont pris soin d'appesantir sur les conséquences fatales d'un génie essentiellement personnel; et il serait bien possible aussi, après tout, que les plus belles expressions du génie, ailleurs que dans le ciel pur . . . ne pussent être obtenues qu'au prix d'un inévitable sacrifice.'

Still, in spite of this unequivocal declaration of faith, it would be a mistake to suppose that Baudelaire admitted any clear distinction between his 'Dandyism' and his poetry. Though he saluted the artistic heroism of Flaubert when *Madame Bovary* appeared, he did not particularly admire it; much less would he have admired the attitude of Cézanne towards his painting or Mr. Hardy towards his poetry. He would have found them lacking in gesture.

Here again Baudelaire was fortunate. The desire for a gesture is not so dangerous in French poetry as it is in English. Traditional French prosody, and above all the prosody of the Alexandrine, is a perpetual invitation to rhetoric, just as the blank verse prosody of Milton sooner or later compels the English poet who adopts it to become more tremendous than he wants to be; but whereas the Miltonic prosody is an aberration from the true English tradition, the prosody of the French Alexandrine is the tradition itself. Wordsworth said of the English sonnet that in Milton's hands 'the thing became a trumpet'; the French poet's difficulty with the Alexandrine has always been to prevent the thing from becoming a trumpet. Luckily Baudelaire wanted a trumpet—one might almost say he wanted a cavalry bugle. The Alexandrine was made for a man possessed by the burning desire to send his challenges ringing up to heaven. Had it not been that his Satanic defiance was moderated by a Satanic sense of *comme il faut*, Baudelaire might have gone the way of Victor Hugo and largely wasted his lesser genius in a mere fury of blowing.

Baudelaire's power of concentration saved him from rhetorical disaster. In the matter of prosody he willingly accepted the severest limitations. He made no technical innovations himself, and he rejected some of those which Victor Hugo had made before him. He saw that for him it was much more important to blow a few blasts that were piercing than many that were merely loud; and he early set himself to the task of finding an equivalent in pure poetry to his detestation of the world and his defiance of the powers that ordained it. He sought the equivalent by making his poetry as metallic in sound and suggestion as he could; he would change the psychological oppression of life into a plastic oppression. To make concrete the immaterial is, of course, a familiar process of the poet's activity, and the effort lies at the source of all metaphor. But Baudelaire went far beyond this phase; he made it his deliberate aim to expel all elasticity from his verse, all bright and ethereal perspectives from his vision. He built himself a house of metal and went from room to room, shutting, bolting, and barring all the magic casements. The surface of his vision and the texture of his verse should alike be hard and impenetrable; thus he would render in poetry his sense of the stifling oppressiveness of life. He would meet steel with steel.

His methods of achieving his end were manifold. The most obvious and the most successful is his endeavour to reduce all living things to a condition of immobile solidity. There is a curious example of this in the *Rêve Parisien*, where the poet dreams of a symbolic landscape:

> Je savourais dans mon tableau
> L'enivrante monotonie
> Du métal, du marbre et de l'eau.

Even at the outset only one-third of his universe—the water—has any chance of moving; within a half a dozen lines he has (literally) petrified even that third.

> Et des cataractes pesantes
> Comme des rideaux de cristal
> Se suspendaient obéissantes
> A des murailles de métal.

Here Baudelaire has indulged his obsession at the cost of an artistic blemish; his stately pleasure-house needed the movement of water to make the contrast of his motionless marble more intense and oppressive. In a poet so scrupulous of his plastic effects the blunder and the underlying motive are the more striking. But in Baudelaire the strangest things are turned to stone and brass; he speaks of a woman's 'granite skin' in one poem, and in the next, 'j'aiguisais lentement sur mon cœur le poignard'. The beautiful Dorothea, his mulatto Venus, is 'belle et froide comme le bronze'. His dreamland of happiness is 'un vrai pays de Cocagne, où tout est riche, propre et luisant, comme une belle conscience, une magnifiquè batterie de cuisine, comme une splendide orfévrerie, comme une bijouterie bariolée'. It is not necessary to accumulate examples; one has but to open *Les Fleurs du Mal* at random to find them. Baudelaire makes solid everything he can. His very ideal of Beauty is an absolute immobility; Beauty itself declares:

> Je hais le mouvement qui déplace les lignes
> Et jamais je ne pleure et jamais je ne ris.

We are not surprised that Beauty should define itself in terms exactly descriptive of the inscrutable Dandy; nor even that an immobile Beauty should be a symbol of the poet's oppression by an adamantine and inexorable world. In Baudelaire's vision of the cosmos, as we have said, steel is opposed to steel. The oppressor and the oppressed are equally ruthless, equally immobile, equally conscious, and equally beautiful. Only the poet-hero knows the Adversary, but to know him is to salute the splendour of his majesty.

> Être maudit à qui, de l'abîme profond
> Jusqu'au plus haut du ciel, rien hors moi ne répond!
> —Ô toi, qui comme une ombre à la trace éphémère,
> Foules d'un pied léger et d'un regard serein
> Les stupides mortels qui t'ont jugé amère,
> Statue aux yeux de jais, grand ange au front d'airain!

To this Moloch of existence the poet sacrifices himself

in an ecstasy which is concealed beneath a mask of bronze. In harmony with the clangour of this meeting of metallic opposites, Baudelaire conceived himself as working like a smith at an anvil on the very words of his poems, hammering and shaping them till they rang with a steely resonance. It is something more than a metaphorical flight when he speaks of

> mes vers polis, treillis d'un pur métal,
> Savamment constellé de rimes de cristal.

That is not fancy, but a precise description of them; they are tempered: and even if the poet had not himself given the hint, one might without any violent exercise of the imagination have compared them to sword-blades, cunningly damascened.

Within this metallic resonance which is the large and general characteristic of Baudelaire's poetry we may distinguish many variations and undertones; or rather we may say that in one continuous and predominant physical sensation—for Baudelaire's verse is physically oppressive—we can detect various separate pulses. Of these the most remarkable might be called an exacerbation of the image. It appears in many forms: in some it is used to give to a vague emotion the acuteness of a physical sensation, as in 'Ces affreuses nuits Qui compriment le cœur comme un papier qu'on froisse'. Sometimes it is a peculiar variation of the dominant endeavour after solidity which has already been discussed. Thus he writes of the beautiful Dorothea:

> Ta gorge qui s'avance et qui pousse la moire,
> Ta gorge triomphante est une belle armoire
> Dont les panneaux bombés et clairs
> Comme les boucliers accrochent des éclairs.

The varieties are, indeed, too many to be separately

defined; but a small collection of examples will show some of the curious tones that Baudelaire extracted from this singular instrument:

> Le ciel! couvercle noir de la vaste marmite
> Où bout l'imperceptible et vaste humanité . . .

> Cœur racorni, fumé comme un jambon . . .

> La nuit s'épaississait ainsi qu'un cloison . . .

> > Sous le fardeau de ta paresse
> > Ta tête d'enfant
> > Se balance avec la mollesse
> > D'un jeune éléphant . . .

> Le plaisir vaporeux, fuira vers l'horizon
> Ainsi qu'une sylphide au fond de la coulisse . . .

> Quand, ainsi qu'un poète, il [le Soleil] descend dans
>   les villes
> Il ennoblit le sort des choses les plus viles . . .

> On voit un chiffonnier qui vient, hochant la tête,
> Buttant et se cognant aux murs comme un poète,
> Et, sans prendre souci des mouchards, ses sujets,
> Épanche tout son cœur en glorieux projets.

Some of these attempted effects may be traced to the desire to astonish which is permitted to the Dandy on the condition that he himself betrays no astonishment. But the explanation would certainly not cover them all, even if the desire to astonish were not closely related to the desire to compel a response, which is not lawful only but essential to the poet. Some of them are curiously beautiful; they have a novel and bizarre beauty that lingers in the mind. The Dandy is not only looking steadily at facts; he is extracting from them some quaint and vivid essence that escapes the duller or more cowardly eye. His world may be hard, repellent even, but it is full of a number of interesting things.

Nevertheless, the importance of these quaint vistas opening on to things grotesque or beautiful must not be exaggerated. Baudelaire's exacerbation of the image was destined to play a considerable part in the subsequent evolution of French poetry, and, at second hand, of our own; but he himself used it sparingly, as one aware that the method was scarcely on a scale with the large effect of solidity at which he aimed. His main road of escape from his iron-walled world lay elsewhere, and was as ample as the prison-house was huge. His symbol of deliverance was the sea. The sea appears as often in his poetry as the metals themselves. It was for him a terrestrial infinite that led 'anywhere out of the world'; and even in that famous and beautiful poem *Le Voyage*, the last of *Les Fleurs du Mal*, when the voyagers have returned with their mournful message that in every corner of the world 'the eternal bulletin' is the same, the poet calls to Death as the great ship's captain. After the failure of all voyages, a voyage remains:

> Ô Mort, vieux capitaine, il est temps! levons l'ancre!
> Ce pays nous ennuie, ô Mort! Appareillons!
> Si le ciel et la mer sont noirs comme de l'encre,
> Nos cœurs que tu connais sont remplis de rayons.

Doubtless, in the constant recurrence of the vision and imagery of the sea throughout Baudelaire's poetry, we may detect the profound impression made upon him as a young man by the voyage on which his perturbed parents sent him to cure his passion for poetry. But the sea is, after all, only a symbol; if he had not found the sea to express his intentions he would have found something else; hardly anything, however, that would have served him so well, or have made so universal an appeal. Even those who know nothing of Baudelaire's disdains

and detestations, and would dismiss his attitude of rebel
lion as a mere theatricality, cannot fail to respond to the
suggestion of his recurrent imagery of the sea. We may
call it a simple or a naïve emotion that finds in a
'splendid ship with white sails crowding' the perfect
symbol of the freedom and happiness that are hidden
beyond our mortal horizon; it is a profound emotion,
and, what is more, an emotion peculiarly of our time.
An age of industrialism drives men to treasure the
symbol of the sea and its ships. Baudelaire made a
magnificent use of this great modern commonplace.
'Grand style: rien de plus beau que les lieux communs',
he notes in his Journal, where we also find this delicate
statement of the fundamental theme:

'Ces beaux et grands navires, imperceptiblement balancés
(dandinés) sur les eaux tranquilles, ces robustes navires, à
l'air désœuvré et nostalgique, ne nous disent-ils par une
langue muette: Quand partons-nous pour le bonheur?'

The image appears in an innumerable variety of forms
and contexts. Music is a sea opening on to he knows not
what freedom:

> Je mets à la voile
> La poitrine en avant et les poumons gonflés
> Comme de la toile.

The lovely Dorothea sails along his memory like a ship.
Again, 'notre âme est un trois-mâts cherchant son
Icarie'. Every desire for the illimitable, every hope that
some final freedom lay behind the brazen wall of circumstance, took concrete form in this image. If in a
rare moment his fascinated loathing of the octopus city
gives place to a delighted contemplation, it is because
the beloved vision has interposed between him and the
reality. 'Les tuyaux, les clochers', have become 'ces

mâts de la cité'. Here finally are two passages from the *Poèmes en Prose*; placed side by side they render exactly the quality of significance which the sea and the ships possessed for the poet's mind:

'Moi seul, j'étais triste, inconcevablement triste. Semblable à un prêtre à qui on arracherait sa divinité, je ne pouvais, sans une navrante amertume, me détacher de cette mer si monstrueusement séduisante, de cette mer si infiniment variée dans son effrayante simplicité, et qui semble contenir en elle et représenter par ses jeux, ses allures, ses colères et ses sourires, les humeurs, les agonies et les extases de toutes les âmes qui ont vécu, qui vivent et qui vivront' (*Déjà*).

'Un port est un séjour charmant pour une âme fatiguée des luttes de la vie. L'ampleur du ciel, l'architecture mobile des nuages, les colorations changeantes de la mer, le scintillement des phares, sont un prisme merveilleusement propre à amuser les yeux sans jamais les lasser. Les formes élancées des navires, au gréement compliqué, auxquels la houle imprime des oscillations harmonieuses, servent à entretenir dans l'âme le goût du rythme et de la beauté, et puis, surtout, il y a une sorte de plaisir mystérieux et aristocratique pour celui qui n'a plus ni curiosité ni ambition, à contempler, couché dans le belvédère ou accoudé sur le môle, tous ces mouvements de ceux qui partent et de ceux qui reviennent, de ceux qui ont encore la force de vouloir, le désir de voyager ou de s'enrichir' (*Le Port*).

The sea is life, and the ship that rides over it is that triumphant, impossible beauty which haunts the mind with the promise that by its power the terrors of life may be overcome. It is only a dream, as Baudelaire well knew, but he dreamed it continually.

For Baudelaire was truly an *âme damnée*, because he was in love with the ideal. The fox of disillusion and disgust really tore at his vitals. Like Ivan Karamazov, he persisted in his determination to give God back the ticket; because his sensitiveness was such that the degradation and misery of life left him no peace. Ennui and spleen had 'magnified themselves into divinities'; they were not petulant and momentary outbreaks of emotionalism, but constant factors of his being. To maintain himself he adopted an attitude, he became Satanic after the pattern of the Miltonic Satan, whom he considered the perfect type of manly beauty; and in the parallel world of art he sought to transform the reactions of his sensibility into the elements of a cosmos of his own making, a little universe that should produce in us the emotions that had tormented him in the world of everyday. Sometimes the original emotions show through the mask he wore; not through any artistic failure on his part, for no man was ever more resolute in his determination to sacrifice himself to his achievement, but because in the later work in prose he was intentionally loosening the rigour of his artistic creed. He was looking for a more precise equivalence to his feeling. In the texture of the *Poèmes en Prose* we can distinguish the separate threads of emotion which are lost in the stiff brocade of *Les Fleurs du Mal*. The prose is more lightly and in a sense more delicately woven; the unity of effect which the little pieces give derives more from complicated harmony than from the resonant unison which marks the poetry. In his prose Baudelaire is content to be ironical, compassionate, lyrical, and symbolic by turns; each piece has the contour of a single mood, together they have the complex solidity of an attitude. There, if we look, we may find as much of Baudelaire the man, as much of his human sensibility, as we shall ever find; there his pity, his irony, his dreams have their original quality, their individuality is not submerged. And there we discover an exquisite compassion and sympathy with the oppressed, of which we may be sure none of those who denounced his immorality was ever remotely capable; and even now few people know that it was Baudelaire who wrote in *Les Veuves* one of the most compassionate phrases in all literature:

'Avez-vous quelquefois aperçu des veuves sur ces bancs solitaires, des veuves pauvres? Qu'elles soient en deuil ou non, il est facile de les reconnaître. D'ailleurs il y a toujours dans le deuil du pauvre quelque chose qui manque, une absence d'harmonie qui le rend plus navrant. *Il est contraint de lésiner sur sa douleur.* Le riche porte la sienne au grand complet.'

'They are compelled to save on their grief.' No wonder the inventor of this phrase gave toys to the waifs of Paris and watched them 'steal away like cats who take the bit you give them far away to eat, having learned to mistrust men', and recorded with a delicate precision the plans four little children were making for their lives; or that the most cynical of all his cynicisms about love is the little story, 'Les Yeux des Pauvres'. The poet and his mistress are sitting outside a new and splendid café. Suddenly he is aware of a poor man holding two tiny children by the hand; all three are staring, 'extraordinarily serious', with large and fascinated eyes into the café:

'Non seulement j'étais attendri par cette famille d'yeux, mais je me sentais un peu honteux de nos verres et de nos carafes, plus grands que notre soif. Je tournais mes regards vers les vôtres, cher amour, pour y lire *ma* pensée; je plongeais dans vos yeux si beaux et si bizarrement doux, dans vos yeux verts, habités par le Caprice et inspirés par la Lune, quand vous me dites: "Ces gens-là sont insuppor-

tables, avec leurs yeux ouverts comme des portes-cochères!
Ne pourriez-vous pas prier le maître du café de les éloigner
d'ici?"

Tant il est difficile de s'entendre, mon cher ange, et tant
la pensée est incommunicable, même entre gens qui s'ai-
ment!'

This suppressed yet passionate sympathy with the
sufferings of the poor is one of the deepest strains in
Baudelaire's nature; it helps to give to his ennui and
his spleen the decisive, creative force which a passing
mood of disenchantment could never have. Unlike
Verlaine, Baudelaire is a constructive poet; he works
from a constant centre and builds on a firm foundation.
It was easy for Verlaine to react against his first admiration for Baudelaire and say, 'Prends l'éloquence et tords-
lui son cou'. He had very little to be eloquent about;
but Baudelaire's moods have all the force of convictions,
they have the backing of an accumulation of unfor-
gotten injuries. Even when he is deliberately striving
to express a mood, the effect is massive and overwhelming. To compare with Verlaine's plaintive songs his
Chant d'Automne:

> Bientôt nous plongerons dans les froides ténèbres;
> Adieu, vive clarté de nos étés trop courts!
> J'entends déjà tomber avec des chocs funèbres
> Le bois retentissant sur le pavé des cours.

is to apprehend 'the difference between poetry of an
eternal intensity and poetry that is merely beautiful'.
The grave austerity of *Recueillement* belongs to the same
rare order of achievement, the highest of which French
poetry is capable:

> Sois sage, ô ma Douleur, et tiens-toi plus tranquille.
> Tu réclamais le soir; il descend; le voici.

There were one or two enthusiastic critics who wel-

comed the appearance of *Les Fleurs du Mal* with references to the great name of Dante. They were generous;
but their instinct was sound. Baudelaire stands to Dante
in a relation not unlike that of Keats to Shakespeare.

We need not describe in detail the misery of the poet's
life. Behind his mask he waged an incessant but a losing
battle against a strange paralysis of the will. Only in
the last two years, during which his letters to his mother
and the fragments of his intimate journal have been
published, has it been possible to appreciate his sufferings. Even now much of his life remains mysterious; but
enough is revealed to show how striking are the points
of resemblance between him and Dostoevsky. The two
men were born in the same year. Certainly Baudelaire's
powers were less than those of the Russian, but had
Dostoevsky died when Baudelaire did, in 1867, he would
have left only *Crime and Punishment* of his greater novels.
Baudelaire did not live to push his exploration into the
possibilities of rebellion so far. But Dostoevsky would
have found in him all the material for one of his inscrutable heroes. This heroic side of Baudelaire, his
prolonged and passionate attempt to live up to his own
conception of heroism, is the part of his private life
which most excites our curiosity, for it has a direct
bearing upon his work as a poet. We may take his
actual existence in the underworld for granted, as we
take Dostoevsky's; it is his endeavour to establish himself in a place midway between the *âme supérieure* of his
compatriot Stendhal and the Stavrogin of Dostoevsky
that needs illumination. In his journals we catch only
fitful glimpses of his immense exercise of will. We grasp
at odd, fragmentary phrases like 'Self-purification and
Anti-Humanity' (written in English and in big letters),
or 'Être un grand homme et un saint pour lui-même,

voilà l'unique chose importante', or this—with its
curious anticipation of an uncanny scene in *The Possessed*
—'Le Dandy doit aspirer à être sublime sans interruption: il doit vivre et dormir devant un miroir.' And
how unexpected to those who persist, like Mr. Arthur
Symons in his recent study, in seeing in Baudelaire only
a Swinburnian singer of 'strange sins', will this be! 'Il
ne peut y avoir du progrès (vrai, c'est-à-dire moral) que
dans l'individu et par l'individu lui-même.' Yet all
these professions of faith are perfectly consistent. Baudelaire's pursuit of the ideal of the rebellious angel called
for a rigorous self-discipline and aimed at an ethical
victory; but it also demanded enormous courage and
physical endurance. The isolation of the man who
adopts an individualist morality is complete; he cannot
expect sympathy or even understanding. Even a friend
and admirer like Théophile Gautier confessed that he
knew nothing about Baudelaire the man. We see the
evidence of the tortures which he suffered from his
spiritual loneliness in the almost hysterical way in which
he clung to the affection of his mother and of Jeanne
Duval, to both of whom he was, and knew he was, quite
incomprehensible.

'One cannot live in rebellion,' said Ivan Karamazov.
Just as Baudelaire used the symbol of the sea in his
poetry for a way of escape from the adamantine world
he had made, so in his life he was haunted by the
thought that a simple domesticity might liberate him
from the oppression and fascination of Paris. He will
live in suburban rusticity with Jeanne at Neuilly in a
quiet little 'home'—it is the English word he uses; and
nothing is more pathetic than his hysterical attempts
to escape to his mother's villa in Honfleur. Again and
again the plans are made, the day fixed. In vain. A

month or more of silence precedes the inevitable letter, with its pages of feverish explanation why it was impossible. When he did break away from Paris, it was only to be drawn into the vortex of another great city; and when at last he made the journey from Brussels to Honfleur his mother herself brought him, for he was paralysed and speechless.

So, too, in his inward consciousness he dreamed of a way of escape by belief in God. In his moments of doubt of his own endurance came the thought that there still might be an explanation of all that was intolerable to him in life: the veil of the mystery might be lifted. We have for evidence the pitiful prayers which are scattered through his Journal, and the appeal with which he ends *Mademoiselle Bistouri*:

'La ville fourmille de monstres innocents.—Seigneur, mon Dieu! vous le Créateur, vous, le Maître; vous qui avez fait la Loi et la Liberté; vous, le Souverain qui laissez faire, vous le Juge qui pardonnez; vous qui êtes plein de motifs et de causes, et qui avez peut-être mis dans mon esprit le goût de l'horreur pour convertir mon cœur, comme le guérison au bout d'une lame; Seigneur, ayez pitié, ayez pitié des fous et des folles! Ô Créateur! peut-il exister des monstres aux yeux de Celui-là seul qui sait pourquoi ils existent, comment ils *se sont faits* et comment ils auraient pu ne pas se faire?'

'Healing at the point of the knife.' Baudelaire was never to believe it wholly, but it was a possibility which haunted him. Perhaps it weakened his resolution; certainly it was a cause of that paralysis of the will—the faculty by which he chiefly lived—which most afflicted him in his later days. The poignant notes in his Journal, 'Travail immédiat, même mauvais, vaut mieux que la rêverie', his repeated references to 'le sentiment du gouffre', give us an inkling of what he endured.

Baudelaire was a great poet of a decadence. In other words, he was a great modern poet; for the decadence which shaped him by compelling him to revolt against it was the 'civilization of industrial progress' which has endured from his day to our own. Baudelaire confronted the reality like the hero he strove to be; he had the courage both of his attitude and his art, and the result of his unremitting exercise of will in transforming his keen emotions is a poetic achievement that makes a single and profound impression upon our minds. Baudelaire, true to the practice of the great poet, had crystallized his experience; he had accumulated a weight of conviction to endorse his emotions. 'Dans certains états de l'âme presque surnaturels' (he wrote), 'la profondeur de la vie se révèle tout entière dans le spectacle, si ordinaire qu'il soit, qu'on a sous les yeux. Il en devient le symbole.' We have tried to elucidate the quality which Baudelaire discerned in 'the depth of life' and to disentangle some of the methods by which he sought to convey it to posterity. He was indeed the poet of rebellion; but the resolution of his defiance was subtly modulated by doubts and dreams which he would entertain and cherish for a while and then dismiss with an ironical contempt for his own unworthy weakness. Underneath his steely surface lay an infinity of sensitive responses. We could have deduced it; deep resentments are born only of deep wounds, and the solidity of permanent poetry is the work only of the most delicate fingers. But the finest artist seldom permits the precise quality of his personal response to appear. He makes his sacrifice to his own universality. It is for us to detect where most the man shows through the texture of his work; and we may decide that Baudelaire reveals himself nowhere more plainly than in these last two stanzas of *L'Irréparable*:

J'ai vu parfois au fond d'un théâtre banal
   Qu'enflammait l'orchestre sonore,
Une fée allumer dans un ciel infernal
   Une miraculeuse aurore;
J'ai vu parfois au fond d'une théâtre banal

Un être, qui n'était que lumière, or et gaze,
   Terrasser l'énorme Satan;
Mais mon cœur, que jamais ne visite l'extase,
   Est un théâtre où l'on attend
Toujours, toujours en vain, l'Être aux ailes de gaze.

[MARCH 1921.

X

AMIEL

'IF we look,' says Benedetto Croce at the end of the most suggestive chapter of his book on the writing of history, 'merely at the enormous amount of psychological observations and moral doubts accumulated in the course of the nineteenth century by poetry, fiction, and the drama, those voices of our society, and consider that in great part it remains without critical treatment, some idea can be formed of the immense amount of work that it falls to philosophy to accomplish.' Whether the traditionalist would call the work that Croce indicates philosophy or history or criticism is of no particular account; what is important is that it remains to be done. Until it is done the twentieth century will always be liable to be puffed up with a conceit of its superiority to a century which it has not yet troubled to understand.

It is true there are signs in England of a fashionable reversion to the Victorian era; it is being exhibited as a curiosity with patient skill. But the Victorianism which may have a present vogue is a very local and limited variety of the consciousness of the nineteenth century; it does not contain England's contribution to that consciousness. The work of isolating and estimating that contribution is eminently a work of seriousness, and seriousness—the 'spoudaiotês' for which Matthew Arnold so strongly pleaded—is not the quality most frequently demanded or supplied to-day. The very word jars on a modern ear. To be serious is to be solemn, to be solemn portentous. Yet it is silly to approach the England of the Oxford Movement, of Clerk-Maxwell, and Huxley, and Arnold, of Thomas Hardy, in a superficial mood. The depths of these men were troubled. If we can see their agonies only as grimaces, we had better leave them alone.

But the time will come, and the work will be done. Not until the twentieth century is fully aware of the nineteenth and has exerted itself to put a valuation upon its achievement, will it have the strength for an achievement of its own. When the work is being done and nineteenth century England is being seen in its true relation to the European consciousness of the period, Henri-Frédéric Amiel will be one of the landmarks in the survey. He may even be a basis for the triangulation, as a piece of flat, unbroken, compact ground serves best for the certain measurement of the great peaks on the horizon.

The nineteenth century was complex and titanic, a *saeculum mirabile* if ever there was one, a century difficult to comprehend by reason of the magnitude of the peaks that rose from it. In it Amiel appears like one of those little convex mirrors which reflect, in bright and distinct minuscule, the colossal landscape on to which the window opens. All the potentialities are there, none of the realizations. He is a microcosm of the moral effort and moral perturbation of a century in which moral effort and perturbation reached a climax. Now that we are in the trough of the wave, weary and impatient beforehand of the attempt to penetrate into the significance of a Tolstoy, a Nietzsche, or a Dostoevsky, it is well that we should have a miniature in Amiel to remind us that this was a pigmy in the days when there were giants.

From the days of Rousseau until the end of the nineteenth century the European mind was concentrated upon a moral problem. It is sometimes said that the

nineteenth century was the century of science; but it was
the moral, the religious, in a word the humane interest
of science which riveted men's minds. They waited on
tiptoe to see what light science would cast on the
problem of man's place in the universe. It was a century
which accepted the fact that the universe could no
longer be regarded as anthropocentric. It opened with
Rousseau's intoxicated chant of freedom, proclaiming
that 'man was born good'. The paraphernalia of
divinely sanctioned institutions could be swept away
without fear, for the kingdom of Heaven was within
men. Within a few years his uncomprehending disciples
were teaching the world that the kingdom of Hell was
there also.

The problem of the nineteenth century was the
problem of morality without institutions. The institution of the state was reduced to a matter of majorities
and progressively worse educated majorities, the institution of the church to a department of the state or an
antiquarian relic. Religion and morality might possibly
be psychological needs, but they might prove to be
psychological illusions or, at least, no more than psychological habits evolved for the better protection of the
triumphant herd; certainly the structure of the universe
and the processes of animal life provided no endorsement for them. The earth and all that is therein was
a trivial incident in the incomprehensible cosmic adventure. How were men to live? Where was a sanctioned
principle of conduct to be found? In pursuit of the
answer arose that amazing company of 'God-seekers', to
use the simple and impressive Russian name, Tolstoy,
Dostoevsky, Nietzsche, Hardy, or their fellows, like
Baudelaire and Stendhal, who affected the Stoic part
and turned an impassive face on the chaotic and incom-

prehensible world. Whatever their differences, these great figures of the nineteenth century were occupied with a single problem: to discover a morality.

To this company Amiel belonged. Probably he was the smallest and least vigorous among them, but to them he indisputably belonged. With his intellect he accepted the universe of science, with his heart he admitted the necessity of religion and morality. He spent his life trying to find a place for the one in the other. In his intense and unremitting effort to reconcile them he reached strange ecstasies and strange despairs. He sounded in his soul the whole octave of the nineteenth century consciousness and left a record of his experiences in a book which has become, as it deserved to become, a minor classic of the century he lived in.

Amiel lived his life as a professor of aesthetics and philosophy in the Academy of Geneva. He wrote some poetry and translated more; he also wrote a little criticism. But the finest passages of his *Il Penseroso* are so reticent that they need the *Journal* to give them substance, and the best of his deliberate criticism is below the level of the incidental estimates in the *Journal*. All Amiel is there. Only there did his rare and delicate gift of expression find the protective atmosphere in which it could expand; it was not strong enough to endure any but the tempered and incense-laden air of posthumous publication. The true creator does not fear to give hostages to fortune, and to deliver to the mercies of the world books in which is only half his thought and that imperfectly expressed; he risks misunderstanding in the confidence that what is to come will correct the insufficiency of what is past. 'Continuez vos ouvrages,' said Galiani to Madame d'Épinay, 'c'est une preuve d'attachement à la vie que de composer des livres.' But

Amiel was not attached to life; to him the thought of incompleteness and misinterpretation was a perpetual terror; and he chose, in the little work he did publish, rather to conceal than to reveal his thought, and preferred in poetry minutiae of form to adequacy of content.

This horror of exposure which stultified the literary production of his lifetime was only a particular manifestation of the fear of life which marked him from the beginning for its own. In his inward experience it emerged as a terror of moral responsibility. Like all the elements of his composition, in the process of his painfully scrupulous investigation of himself, it assumed the most unlikely disguises. And perhaps the most striking quality of Amiel's introspection—a perfect type of intellectual introspection—is the self-deception it contained. Sometimes, indeed, he had a blindingly clear sight of his own nature, but quite as often the illusion was complete. Time after time he diagnosed his disease as *la maladie de l'idéal.* He was so enamoured of perfection, he believed, that he could not accept the imperfect, so desirous of the whole that he could not be satisfied with the part, whether of knowledge or even of life itself. He could not love for fear his love might be less than the perfect consummation he dreamed of; he could not give himself to work, because to know one thing perfectly meant to know all things. In other words, he refused to be anything less than God. That is, of course, an uncharitable description of a nature so fine as Amiel's; but in a nature so subtle it is peculiarly necessary to separate, even with a blunt and brutal instrument, the part of self-deception from the core of truth. That Amiel was in love with the ideal no one can doubt. Perfect truth, perfect love, perfect beauty, perfect harmony were dreams that truly haunted him.

But it was not the contrast between the poverty of the real and the richness of the ideal that froze the veins of action in him, it was 'thinking too precisely on the event'; it was fear.

The *malade de l'idéal* is a *malade imaginaire*. The ideal, if it is present to a mind at all, as it was to Amiel's, is a spur, not an obstacle, to action. When it is put forward as the cause of inaction, we may be sure that the diagnosis is romantic and untrue. It recurs continually in the earlier portion of Amiel's *Journal*, but it disappears in the later years. Then Amiel recognized that his disease was fear. He was afraid of the menacing universe which his mind held before him: he was devoured by the misgiving that every act was a mere venturing of the hand into the spinning cogwheels of the huge, implacable machine—'l'engrenage terrible de la souffrance humaine et la responsabilité humaine'—just as in the microcosm of literature he felt that to express his thoughts was only to draw the clumsy misinterpretations of a hostile criticism upon his head. It was a consciousness of the sheer danger of living that drove him back upon himself; he peeped out of his tiny window on to the grim waste of life, unlit by any purpose, and he drew back in dismay.

Amiel could not take the plunge into life, not because it was imperfect, but because it was cruel. This was the fundamental verity in the man. What is of absorbing and permanent interest are the strange metamorphoses which this fear underwent in the crucible of his intellect. Melancholy and diffidence were familiar to the human spirit long before the Copernican revolution; probably *taedium vitae* is as old as humanity. The conviction that the universe is mechanical and therefore indifferent only opened a new chapter in the history of the 'ennui

commun à toute personne bien née'. The distinction
between the instinct and the intellect of Amiel is therefore logical rather than psychological. His intellectual
apprehension of the indifference of the universe was the
nurse, though not the parent, of his fear.

It was natural that the effort to overcome this fear
in the realm of the intellect should hold the chief place
in Amiel's record of his inward struggles. The process
of the intellect is clear; a man's deeper evolution is not.
Besides, he had somehow to *prove* that the universe was
not indifferent. That was impossible as it has always
been. An inward *change* is necessary, as Dostoevsky
knew when he created Alyosha. But that inward change,
in spite of all his passing self-deceptions, was impossible
for Amiel to achieve, and it may even be that in this
one respect his analysis was keener than that of the great
Russian. Amiel tried to accept the process of becoming,
of birth and death and pain in the universe, as a mighty
and indivisible whole. It was one; therefore, surely, it
was a harmony. Man could fall down and worship it,
he could acknowledge in his soul that, like a great work
of art, it could not be otherwise. To take away the
suffering and the evil would be to separate the warp from
the woof of the sublime pattern. Man could bow himself, not ignobly, not without joy, to this vision of
necessity. Who can tell whether it was not this doubtful
beatitude which entered Alyosha's soul when he fell
upon the earth and wept at the vision of harmony?
We do not know what lay in store for Dostoevsky's
latest hero.[1]

But Amiel, who knew this condition of frozen ecstasy,
also knew that it was not real acceptance.

'Il n'y a pas de paix que dans la réconciliation avec la

---

[1] See note, p. 192.

destinée, quand la destinée paraît religieusement bonne,
c'est-à-dire quand l'homme se sent directement en présence
de Dieu. Alors seulement la volonté acquiesce. Elle n'acquiesce même tout à fait que lorsqu'elle adore. L'âme ne
se soumet aux duretés du sort qu'en découvrant une com-
pensation magnifique, la tendresse du Tout-Puissant.'—
(*August* 16, 1875.)

Perhaps he never formulated quite clearly to himself
the difference between a true religious acceptance and
the ecstasy of self-immolation on the altar of the cosmic
process; they are extremely subtle states of mind. The
basis of the former is moral, the basis of the other
aesthetic. It may be that language is impotent to
distinguish these impulses in their supreme manifesta-
tions; but they are not the same. Amiel may not have
defined the difference, but he knew it, as doubtless
many saints within and seers without the Christian
Church have known it.

One thing is necessary, Amiel repeats again and
again, *L'abandon à Dieu*. But where and what could
God be for him? Try as he may—and the agony of his
effort is apparent to the least sympathetic reader of his
Journal—to give his Deity substance, he finds him always
dissolving away into the same indifferent and un-
differentiated cosmic process. In his earlier days he
had managed to persuade himself that he could enter
by force of imagination into all beings and forms of life,
and that this illusory expansion of the self was communion with God. When the illusion began to fail he
comforted himself, like the men of Athens, by erecting
an altar to the Unknown God. 'Sois dans l'ordre toi-
même et laisse à Dieu le soin de débrouiller l'écheveau
du monde et des destinées. Qu'importe le néant ou
l'immortalité? Ce qui doit être, sera; ce qui sera, sera

bien.'—(*April* 24, 1869.) There he is on the road to
a pure agnosticism. Three years later his disintoxication
is complete.

'La sagesse consiste à juger le bon sens et la folie, et à se
prêter à l'illusion universelle sans en être dupe. Entrer dans
le jeu de Maïa, faire de bonne grâce sa partie dans la tragi-
comédie fantasque qu'on appelle l'Univers, c'est le plus
convenable pour un homme de goût qui sait folâtrer avec
les folâtres, et être sérieux avec les sérieux.'

To play a game of which you can never know the rules,
to act a part of which you can never know the lines, is
a difficult morality. It is true Amiel goes on to explain
that this is the end of a pure intellectualism, and that
the heart of man can never accept it; but he has nothing
more to offer, and the passage closes on a note of
complete despair.

'L'esprit en tant que pensée arrive à l'intuition que toute
réalité n'est que le rêve d'un rêve. Ce qui nous fait sortir
du palais des songes, c'est la douleur, la douleur personnelle;
c'est aussi le sentiment de l'obligation, ou ce qui réunit les
deux, la douleur du péché; c'est encore l'amour; en un mot
c'est l'ordre moral. Ce qui nous arrache aux enchantements
de Maïa, c'est la conscience. La conscience dissipe les
vapeurs du kief, les hallucinations de l'opium et la placidité
de l'indifférence contemplative. Elle nous pousse dans l'engrenage terrible de la souffrance humaine et de la responsabilité humaine. C'est le réveille-matin, c'est le cri du coq
qui met en fuite les fantômes, c'est l'archange armé du
glaive qui chasse l'homme du paradis artificiel. L'intel-
lectualisme ressemblait à une ivresse qui se déguste; le
moralisme est à jeun, c'est une famine et une soif qui
refusent de dormir. Hélas! Hélas!'

The moral fact, as Amiel elsewhere says, is also a fact.
The consciousness of sin and the longing for duty are
indeed facts. But they are very variable facts which

could offer hardly more resistance to his analysis than
the fact of a divinely ordained universe. Was the notion
of duty to which he clung so desperately more substantial than the straw clutched at by a drowning man?
What was he in fact to do? To play his part in the game
of Maïa? Whatever he did he would be doing that, no
less than the murderer and the liar. To do good to his
neighbour? But what was good? Was it good, for
instance, to tell his students at Geneva the truth about
the Universe as he perceived it? His conscience gave
him no answer to that. To do his part in diminishing
the suffering of the world? To that and nothing more
the duty of the sceptic slowly dwindles down. It is,
indeed, not a little; but, alas, it also may be dissolved
away. Amiel did not choose the method of Dostoevsky's
terrifying heroes who deliberately violated this last
dictate of conscience to see what might happen, and
discover whether the whisper of conscience was only the
last illusion of all. Amiel was not the man to put his
radical scepticism into action; but scepticism itself was
potent enough to dissolve away the duty of diminishing
suffering. The part of suffering in the history of
humanity was undeniable. If it was unnecessary, then
the Universe was either a chaos or the work of a satanic
power; if it was necessary, it was lost labour to try to
diminish it. So the tender-hearted Amiel, to whom in
his youth war had seemed the last futility of a blind
ignorance, was driven at the last into the hateful position
of justifying war.

'Les maudisseurs de la guerre ressemblent à ceux maudis-
sent la foudre, les orages ou les volcans; ils ne savent ce
qu'ils font. La civilisation tend à pourrir les hommes,
comme les grandes villes à vicier l'air. *Nos patimur longae
pacis mala.*'—(*March* 20, 1880.)

These are the very accents of the philosophers of militarism. On the lips of Amiel, a year before his death, they sound strangely indeed.

Thus the last duty of man turned to ashes. Amiel spent his life in obeying a conscience he could not believe in, and fulfilling a duty that was meaningless to him. Everything he touched with those timid, delicate, reverential fingers crumbled into dust. The words remained, but the substance was lost.

'L'être moral peut moraliser ses souffrances en utilisant le fait naturel pour son éducation intérieure. Ce qu'il ne peut changer, il l'appelle la volonté de Dieu, et vouloir ce que Dieu veut lui rend la paix.'—(*September* 1, 1874.)

Again it is the unsubstantial God of a pure agnosticism. Though he may have deceived himself for the moment he knew there was no peace to be found in that submission. Not a year had passed before he declared that 'il n'y a pas de paix que lorsque la destinée paraît religieusement bonne'. A destiny which consists only in the things which we long to change but cannot, and a God whose single attribute it is that he wills those things, were not to be worshipped by Amiel; he could not so far abrogate his humanity.

Nothing but Stoic renunciation was left. The word 'God' emptily reverberates through the last pages of his *Journal*. By some curious process of self-hallucination he declared to the last that he believed in God; but it was an assertion of the desire to believe, not of belief. He was utterly cast out from life; his rebellion had ended in nihilism, his promise in disaster. He thought back on what he had done. Nothing. *Omnis moriar*, he wrote bitterly. Let us hope that even then he knew that the record of his seeking was imperishable. Centuries hence, when the struggles and disenchantments and despairs of the nineteenth century may be no more real than the vague memory of an uneasy dream, Amiel will be known and loved and pitied.

Perhaps the healthy and tough-minded pity him now, if they read him. But their pity is more likely to be the pity of ignorance than understanding. Amiel's travail of mind cannot be thrust aside. It does not belong to the past, but to the present, and still more to the future. Men have discovered God in our own day. But it is doubtful whether the Invisible King is more substantial than Amiel's Maïa. God, to be God, must be seen and known and loved, or he is no more than eternal illusion, a romantic expansion of the self into a universe which is not self at all. On the one side there is religion, which can abate nothing of its claim to a truly personal God; on the other side there is an indifferent universe. Amiel's *Journal* is a demonstration that will hold good for all time that the attempt to find a third way between these opposites is a barren self-deception.[1]

The search for a morality remains, unsatisfied; it even seems that it is neglected now as an unfashionable relic of a bygone era. The misty religion of the new evangelists will not provide one; and the new psychology is so interpreted that it is become a mere corrosive of responsibility. Nevertheless, an intellectual age which neglects morality will itself be neglected, for the desire to be good is one of the deepest longings of the human heart. Without the discipline of morality life wastes itself in the desert sands. A culture which is blind to this necessity is inevitably futile; it has lost the power of seeing life steadily and whole, it has lost the driving force of the creative passion which springs only from a deep

---

[1] See note, p. 192.

acknowledgement that morality is essential to the conduct of human life. The strength of a truly great writer endures either because he builds upon the foundations of a morality which he accepts, or because he is animated by the intense desire to discover one. The greatest writers, as Tchehov said, have always had axes to grind.

Amiel's title to remembrance rests in the last resort upon his profound conviction of the necessity of morality. However dark the nihilism into which his analysis led him, he proclaimed the truth that 'le fait moral est aussi un fait'. The moral fact, it is true, was the desire for morality and not a morality, as his declaration of belief in God was a declaration of his desire to believe, not of belief. But he saw also that 'la civilisation est surtout une chose morale'. That is to say, he never lost touch with the prime reality of life. It is this moral preoccupation which gives dignity and significance to his *Journal*. Matthew Arnold's failure to respond to this dominant quality in Amiel makes his essay irrelevant and superficial. That Amiel had a singularly acute critical intuition is true, though Arnold managed to miss the finest manifestation of it. Amiel's analysis of Chateaubriand's relation to Rousseau belongs to an order of criticism altogether higher than the remarks on Sainte-Beuve which Arnold quoted admiringly. By discovering no more in Amiel than a literary critic who had missed his vocation he came near to proving that he had missed his own.

In the last balance the positive morality of Amiel is purely Stoic, but he was a Stoic who had a clear intuition of the insufficiency of Stoicism. Morality, he knew, was a discipline; he knew also that it was not enough to suffer the discipline: he must surrender himself to it. This act of surrender was impossible to him, but he thought he saw how it might be achieved without disloyalty to the truth his intellect declared to him.

'L'amour sublime, unique, invincible, mène tout droit au bord du grand abîme, car il parle immédiatement d'infini et d'éternité. Il est éminemment religieux. Il peut même devenir religion. Quand tout autour de l'homme chancelle, vacille, tremble et s'obscurcit dans les lointaines obscurités de l'inconnu, quand le monde n'est plus que fiction et féerie et l'univers que chimère, quand tout l'édifice des idées s'évanouit en fumée et que toutes les réalités se convertissent en doute, quel point fixe peut encore rester à l'homme? C'est le cœur fidèle d'une femme. C'est là qu'on peut appuyer sa tête, pour reprendre du courage à la vie, de la foi en Providence, et, s'il le faut, pour mourir en paix avec la bénédiction sur les lèvres. Qui sait si l'amour et sa béatitude, cette évidente manifestation d'une harmonie universelle des choses, n'est pas la meilleure démonstration d'un Dieu souverainement intelligent et paternel, comme elle est le plus court chemin pour aller à lui? L'amour est une foi et une foi appelle l'autre. Cette foi est une félicité, une lumière, et une force. On n'entre que par là dans la chaîne des vivants, des réveillés, des heureux, des rachetés, des vrais hommes qui savent ce que vaut l'existence et qui travaillent à la gloire de Dieu et de la vérité. Jusque-là on ne fait que babiller, bredouiller, perdre ses jours, ses facultés et ses dons, sans but, sans joie réelle, comme un être infirme, invalide, inutile et qui ne compte pas.'

'It can even become religion.' When we have sifted away all the contradictions in Amiel, this positive indication alone is left in our hands; when we have followed him along all the paths by which he sought peace in vain, this road alone remains open through 'the high, uno'erleaped mountains of necessity'. It was Amiel's bitter fate that he could not enter upon it.

[AUGUST 1921.

XI

AMIEL'S LOVE STORY

I T is common knowledge that hitherto but a fraction
of the whole of Amiel's *Journal* has been published.
The original manuscript, now in the care and control
of M. Bernard Bouvier, contains 16,900 pages. Recently
M. Bouvier published three further volumes of selections;
now he, with the collaboration of M. Edmond Jaloux
and M. Charles Du Bos, has given to the world yet
another substantial volume, of cardinal interest to lovers
or students of Amiel.[1] It consists of those portions of the
Journal which deal with Amiel's relations to women, and
chiefly to one particular woman, whom Amiel discreetly
named Philine, or X, or Hg. Amiel met her, after some
correspondence, in 1859, and for the ensuing twelve
years their relations were extremely intimate, though
not in the cant sense of the common phrase. Philine
became Amiel's lover on one sole occasion, in October
1860, the only occasion when Amiel had experience of
physical love. But for many years he was on the brink,
or what he supposed to be the brink, of marrying her.
He withdrew his timid foot, and died as he had lived,
celibate.

M. Jaloux, in his admirable introduction, gives us
some of Philine's letters to Amiel. They are unmistakable evidence of a passionate devotion to him. Philine
was a young widow who had endured a painful past;
moreover, according to the rigid classifications of the
Genevan *bourgeoisie*, she was not quite Amiel's social
equal. This was one of the excuses he seized upon to

[1] PHILINE. Fragments inédits du Journal Intime de *H. F. Amiel*.
Publiés par *Bernard Bouvier*. Introduction d'*Edmond Jaloux*.

justify to himself his refusal to marry her, though
naturally, since he was Amiel, it took the form of a refusal
to expose her to the gossip of Genevan society and the
hostility of his own family. In this he was no doubt
sincere. Difference in social rank had, in such a situation, little real influence with him; he was genuinely
afraid of the inevitable complications. But the root of
the matter lay deeper, in his radical fear of life, not in
his fear of this particular manifestation of life.

Hence the absorbing interest of this volume of his
Journal. It reveals Amiel's weakness, or Amiel's self, as
it were at the centre; for love and marriage, as he well
knew, are the forms under which life chiefly makes its
demand upon the individual that he should be prepared
to sacrifice his individuality. At this point a man must
risk himself in that mysterious process of which Amiel
had an almost superstitious dread: 'l'engrenage terrible
de la souffrance humaine et de la responsabilité humaine.'
About this fearful machinery Amiel fluttered like a
fascinated bird. Isolated, sensitive, delicately understanding, he longed to be delicately understood; he was
for ever seeking for love, and, as was inevitable with
such a nature, he aroused not a little of it. But what
he aroused would not remain delicate, silken, and
Platonic; he discovered, to his incessant dismay, that
love is passionate and primeval, however frail may be
the vehicle in which it is embodied. 'Une femme com-
prise,' he wailed, 'se croit une femme aimée.' He
managed, quite often, to convince himself that this was
altogether unreasonable, and that the ideal woman
would lend herself freely to his penchant for soul-
investigation without being in the least disturbed by
his inquiries. He reached the comfortable conclusion
that a man, if he does not love more, 'loves better' than

a woman. But 'loving better', if we look closer, simply meant, in Amiel's thinking, loving with detachment. He begged the question.

Amiel knew it. There was, indeed, very little about himself that Amiel did not know. Those who are well acquainted with his *Journal* are familiar with the rhythmical regularity with which first he persuasively justifies himself for a certain attitude, and then, a little more persuasively, at a few days' interval—time enough to have forgotten his previous self-defence—tears his own justification to shreds. In the record of his relations with Philine the phenomenon is remarkable. Whenever he has complained of her lack of 'limpidity', her failure to meet his frankness with an equal frankness, or his consistency with an equal consistency, the moment inevitably follows when he accuses himself bitterly for his cowardice in refusing the life which she had to give, and longed to give. Though there are moments when one feels a robust impatience with him, it is impossible to blame him. That same fundamental terror of life which made him draw back frightened from the flame that he had kindled had driven him to seek consolation and companionship in women's love. He could not bear his own loneliness; neither could he bear the breaking-down of that loneliness in the only way that was possible for him. 'Ma nature est ainsi faite', he wrote at the beginning of his relation with Philine, 'elle s'ingénie à faire le désert autour d'elle, et ne peut souffrir le désert.'

So he poured himself into enchanted feminine ears, in the belief that he could thus escape his own isolation yet still remain isolated. He would, so to speak, face life on the narrowest possible front; and then he was astonished and pained to discover that the whole force of life was concentrated behind a single woman. What she required of him was precisely what life as a whole had been requiring of him; but whereas in the general conduct of his affairs he could find plausible excuses for himself, in the particular instance it was more difficult. He felt that he was not playing fair; he was not giving as good as he got; and, since his conscience, like his consciousness, was acute, he was miserable about it. His general failure he could explain away conveniently enough in metaphysical terms: it was his belief in Maïa that prevented him from action, and by refraining from action he did no harm. But now his weakness appeared to him without metaphysical disguise, in personal terms. He, the kind and sensitive Amiel, was inflicting suffering upon another human being—suffering for which he was wholly responsible. He had indulged himself and brought Philine to a condition of soul of which love and marriage were the rightful consummation. Then he shrank away. His conscience never ceased to accuse him.

As ever with Amiel, he had perfectly clear glimpses of the true situation almost from the beginning. The entries in the *Journal* in October, 1860, are extraordinarily illuminating. On the 6th he had been, for the first and only time in his life, Philine's lover. Immediately afterwards he wrote:

'Mais comment dois-je appeler l'expérience de ce soir? Est-ce une déception, est-ce un enivrement? Ni l'un ni l'autre. J'ai eu pour la première fois une bonne fortune, et franchement, à côté de ce que l'imagination se figure ou se promet, c'est peu de chose. C'est quasi un seau d'eau fraîche. J'en suis bien aise. Cela m'a refroidi en m'éclairant. La volupté elle-même est aux trois quarts ou plus encore dans le désir, c'est-à-dire dans l'ima_ination. La poésie vaut infiniment mieux que la réalité. Mais l'intérêt

vif de l'expérience est essentiellement intellectuel; je puis
enfin raisonner sur la femme, sciemment, sans cette demi-
niaiserie de l'ignorance, ou cette idéalisation fautive de la
pensée, qui m'ont gêné jusqu'ici. Je vois le sexe entier avec
le calme d'un mari, et je sais maintenant que, pour moi du
moins, la femme physique n'est presque rien. La moralité
de l'histoire, c'est que l'affection, la sympathie, l'attachement d'une femme est bien son tout, et que sa faveur dernière ne grossit pas notablement (et à peine sensiblement)
son compte. Quant à la femme même, cela ne m'a autant
appris que je l'espérais. En dernière analyse, je suis stupé-
fait de l'insignifiance relative de ce plaisir dont on fait tant
de bruit ...'

It is an astonishing piece of self-revelation. In spite
of Amiel's disclaimer it is an almost perfect example of
demi-niaiserie; but still more wonderful is the underlying
and uncriticized assumption that he now knew all that
was to be known about physical love. The notion that,
if it was indeed so insignificant a thing as he had found
it, the general attitude of humanity towards it was inexplicable seems not to have entered his head. His
naïve presumption brings to mind the youthful scorn of
Hippolytus and the fearful vengeance exacted by the
dread Queen.

But Amiel was psychologically incapable of physical
love. That something deeper was at work to disturb
his facile intellectual conclusions the note of four days
later is witness:

'Comme l'estomac et les poumons réclament impérieuse-
ment la nourriture de l'air, un autre de nos systèmes
organiques réclame insolemment sa pâture et se moque de
nos réticences comme de nos objections. L'instinct du sexe
travaille en nous sans nous; la nature nous somme de satis-
faire ses droits, ses vœux, ses ordres. Son but ici, c'est la
cessation de la vie individuelle, et l'entrée dans la vie

générique, l'identification avec un autre. Cette combustion
de l'égoïsme, cet abandon de l'individualité, cet oubli total
du moi, je ne l'ai éprouvé dans sa douceur que par l'admiration poétique et par l'émotion intellectuelle ou morale; mais
jamais, je crois, jusqu'au fond de l'être, jusqu'aux moelles.
Ni l'extase, ni la pâmoison, ni l'ivresse, ni l'étourdissement
ne m'ont encore arraché à la conscience de moi-même, ne
m'ont vaincu, anéanti, absorbé; j'ignore la transhumanisa-
tion, et je ne connais que l'impersonnalisation.'

Here Amiel came close, perhaps as close as he ever
came, to acknowledging that the fault lay in himself.
The reality of what is *en nous sans nous* he could not truly
admit. He could admit it as a fact intellectually appre-
hended; he could even admit that in the scheme of
things it had a right to be and fulfilled a function and
a purpose; but to submit himself to it was impossible.
The ecstasy of self-annihilation, he said, had not visited
him; he chose not to remember that the ecstasy visits
no one who is not prepared to receive it. One cannot
stipulate the terms upon which one will receive life.
Sooner or later the demand comes, in one or other of
a thousand forms, that we must lose our life to save it.

Amiel could not suffer it to be so. In his infinite
sophistication he told himself that he could obey nothing
but an irresistible impulse; but to a completely conscious
man, as Amiel was, no impulse is irresistible, not even
the impulse to maintain complete self-consciousness.
There is a very deep self-deception in his final conclusion
after the years-long debate whether he should or should
not marry Philine. He was writing in 1878, nearly
twenty years after their first meeting.

'J'en conclus qu'un mariage n'est à conseiller que s'il est
irrésistible. Il ne faut prendre pour époux que l'être néces-
saire. Dans ce cas, quelle que soit l'issue, on peut se dire:

c'était écrit, c'était mon destin! Dieu l'a voulu, résignons-nous. Comme un œuvre d'art ne vaut rien sans inspiration, une décision irréparable ne vaut rien sans un entraînement surnaturel. Il nous faut l'illusion que Dieu y a mis la main . . .'

It is the voice of an inheritor of centuries of Calvinism. Election is necessary, even in marriage, and Amiel is not of the elect. Indeed, we are inclined to believe that the only complete explanation of Amiel is to be found in his theological inheritance. For we have to explain not only his shrinking from action, but his immense and unique perseverance in composing his *Journal*. To act, to venture himself in the 'engrenage terrible', he needed the grace of God: more of the grace than another because he was aware of more of the dangers. The grace was never vouchsafed to him. But to do nothing, in the moral sense, was impossible. Somehow, somewhere, he had to surrender himself to destiny, and to perform a heroic task. His *Journal* was the opportunity. Only a man of extreme conscience and unconquerable will could have accomplished it. We cannot measure Amiel by common standards, for what we must deny him as a man we must give him again as a writer; and even that separation is finally untenable. It needed nothing less than a hero to make so ruthless a record of his own timidities.   [1929.

XII

GUSTAVE FLAUBERT, 1821–1880

THERE are two Flauberts. One was born on the 12th of December, 1821, in the surgeon's house at Rouen hospital; the other in enthusiastic minds in the last quarter of the nineteenth century. One was a broad, big-boned, lovable, rather simple-minded man, with the look and the laugh of a farmer, who spent his life in agonies over the intensive culture of half a dozen curiously assorted volumes; the other was an incorporeal giant, a symbol, a war-cry, a banner under which a youthful army marched and marches still to the rout of the bourgeois and the revolution of literature.

To distinguish these beings from each other is not so difficult as to understand how they came to be so completely interfused that the separation of the legend and the reality may appear an act of wanton iconoclasm. So much has been derived from the legendary Flaubert, so many advancing waves have borne his name on the crest of their attack, that he has acquired the dignity of an institution. We have a critic of the stature of Remy de Gourmont declaring that Flaubert is the very archetype of the creative writer, for two reasons; because he devoted his life and his personality to his work, suffering nothing to be wasted in the exigencies and delights of mere living, and because he was pre-eminently gifted with visual imagination.

It is not easy to see why the value of a writer's work should depend upon the completeness of his incineration on the altar of Art. A good writer has to make sacrifices, of course, but he need not (indeed, he had better not) burn himself to ashes. Greater writers than Flaubert

have not felt the necessity. To one who is not a born
Flaubertian the astonishing tortures he inflicted upon
himself would naturally suggest, not that his genius was
pre-eminent, but that his creative impulse was not of
the strongest. While the truth about his visual imagination is that it was not of the finest quality. Flaubert
adored images; he believed, truly enough, that the
highest poetic faculty is mastery of metaphor; he fancied
that when he was wholly free to write what pleased
him—though when was he not?—he would triumphantly indulge his passion. Yet, in fact, Flaubert's use
of imagery is almost invariably strained or commonplace, and often both. Take the similes with which
L'Éducation Sentimentale begins and ends: neither is successful. Here is the first:

'Enfin le navire partit; et les deux berges, peuplées de
magasins, de chantiers et d'usines, filèrent comme deux
larges rubans qu'on déroule.'

The image is forced, and it gives the wrong tempo to
the opening movement. A torpedo-boat destroyer could
not steam fast enough to justify it wholly, and this was
a river-steamer on the Seine. The second simile is used
by Madame Arnoux when she revisits Frédéric Moreau:

'Elle s'étonnait de sa mémoire. Cependant, elle lui dit:
— Quelquefois, vos paroles me reviennent comme un
écho lointain, comme le son d'une cloche apporté par le vent:
et il me semble que vous êtes là, quand je lis les passages
d'amour dans les livres.'

This is, indeed, not a visual image; but its discrepancy
is not less remarkable for that. Had the words been
given to the second-rate romanticism of Emma Bovary
they might have been in place. But Madame Arnoux
was designed to be Emma's opposite. For the sake of

a worn-out poetical metaphor, Flaubert was willing to make his heroine speak out of character. It would be hard to find an absolutely convincing metaphor in the whole of his work. Some of them are really comic, as this of Rosanette. 'Toutes ces images qu'elle se créait lui faisait comme autant de fils qu'elle aurait perdus, *l'excès de la douleur multipliant sa maternité. . . .*'

The fact is that Flaubert did not possess the very finest kind of literary discrimination. He had an un-usual visual faculty which he turned to good account, but the use he made of it was primitive. Most of his descriptions are visual pageantry, sometimes impressive, sometimes beautiful, sometimes as tedious as the tail-end of a Lord Mayor's show when we are waiting to cross the Strand. Of the faculty which employs visual imagery to differentiate the subtler emotions of the soul, Flaubert had little or nothing at all. The true faculty of metaphor was denied him.

Lacking this, a writer cannot be reckoned among the greatest masters of style. But Flaubert lacked something more fundamental still. If we consider his works in the order in which they were written we are chiefly struck by the strange absence of inward growth which they reveal. The surface texture of *L'Éducation Sentimentale* is more closely woven than that of *Madame Bovary*, but the scope of the story itself is, if anything, less significant. Flaubert's vision of life had not deepened in the long interval which separates the two works. He saw a larger extent of life, perhaps, but he saw no farther into it; he had acquired more material, but no greater power of handling it; he manipulated more characters, but he could not make them more alive. Though the epicure of technical effects may find more to interest him in the later book, it is impossible not to endorse the general verdict that

Madame Bovary is Flaubert's masterpiece. Undoubtedly the choice lies between those books, for *La Tentation de Saint Antoine* and *Salammbô* are set-pieces which will not kindle, and *Bouvard et Pécuchet* (which Remy de Gourmont declared the equal of *Don Quixote*!) cannot be redeemed from dullness by the mildly amusing bubbles which float to the surface of its viscous narrative.

We may suspect that a writer who does not really develop, the vitality and significance of whose latest work is less than that of his first, has not the root of the matter in him. And Flaubert had not. It may not be given to mortal men to understand life more deeply at the end than at the beginning of their share of it; but they can more keenly feel its complexity and its wonder; they can attain to an eminence from which they contemplate it calmly and undismayed. The great writers do this, and convey the issue of their contemplation to us through the created world which they devise. But of this unmortified detachment Flaubert was incapable. He lived and died indignant at the stupidity of the human race. As he was at thirty, so he was at sixty; in stature of soul he was a young man.

'Récriminer,' asks Baudelaire in *L'Art Romantique*, 'faire de l'opposition, et même réclamer la justice, n'est-ce pas s'emphilistiner quelque peu?' In those three occupations Flaubert spent all his time when he emerged from his *gueuloir*, and it is not too much to say that he was a good deal of a Philistine. He had a bourgeois horror of the bourgeois, and it was this repulsion rather than a natural attraction which kept him chained to his desk at Croisset. Literature was to him an ascetic revenge on life, not a culmination of it; he tore himself up by the roots and planted himself in the most highly artificial atmosphere which a considerable writer has ever breathed. Under this unhealthy stimulation he evolved for himself the doctrine of the sovereign autonomy of art.

He could do no less. Having chosen the ivory tower, he had to justify its existence. Hating life, he had to be convinced that literature was also indifferent to it. Accordingly he tried to persuade himself that the subject-matter of a work of literature was of no account. A structure of beauty could be raised upon no matter what foundation, and beauty was absolute and incommensurable.

Two things are remarkable about this aesthetic theory of Flaubert's; the theory itself, and his manner of holding it. Though it seemed to resemble the doctrine held by other French romantics of his generation, it was profoundly different. Baudelaire, for instance, who claimed for the poet the right to deal with subjects generally held to be immoral, made this claim on behalf of what he considered to be the higher morality of art. He believed that the importance of a subject was independent of the moral estimation in which it was held, but he insisted that the subject should be important. Flaubert, on the other hand, tried to believe that the significance of a subject was an unessential quality. The writer actually endowed it with importance by the beauty of the language in which he treated it. Pressed to its logical conclusion, the theory is almost meaningless, for the writer must choose a subject and must have motives for his choice. So that it is not surprising that Flaubert never wholly satisfied himself. He wavered. At one moment he asserted that 'tout découle de la conception', at another that style was 'the soul beneath the words', at yet another that everything in literature depended on character. These beliefs do not necessarily conflict with one another, but not one of them can really be reconciled with the notion that the subject-matter is indifferent. For some reason Flaubert was incapable of thinking the question out to a conclusion. His formulated theory of writing went no farther than the injunction—valuable enough—to think clearly, express precisely, and read aloud to test the rhythm.

All this he did, and did so well, that our feeling when we contemplate the years he spent upon works so inwardly hollow as *Salammbô*, *La Tentation*, and *Bouvard et Pécuchet*, is one of utter dismay. It seems that it was only by accident that he stumbled on a subject of any significance at all; and indeed it was. It was not the fault of his theory; that had little influence on his practice, and was rather (as most literary theories are) a justification of an accomplished fact. His choice of subjects was governed by his temperament and his temperament was governed by his two predominant emotions: indignation and aversion. Indignation drove him to Yonville and Nogent and Paris; aversion gave him wings to fly to Carthage and the Thebaid. His realism was of disgust, his romanticism of predilection; the realism was in part triumphantly successful, the failure of the romanticism complete. Never was a literary achievement more deeply paradoxical. Flaubert's natural expression was satire, but as we know from *Bouvard et Pécuchet*, and as he himself also recognized, his hand was as heavy in satire as his thought was cumbersome.

Indignation and aversion, unless they find their proper satisfaction in satire, are treacherous emotions for a writer to build on; too frequently they turn to petulance and superficiality. Flaubert was saved from this by the

M 2

qualities of his character. He had an immense capacity
for work, a passionate love of truth, and most important
of all, he worshipped the great writers before him; as he
said, 'he had the bump of veneration strongly developed'.
Though he recognized, with a clearness that should be
disconcerting to his own idolaters, that he was of another
and a lower order than his demigods, he saw that they
had one quality which he too might aim to possess.
They were objective; they did not intrude their personalities into their work; they were content to represent
and to record. Long before he began *Madame Bovary* his
determination to emulate them in this was fixed; when
he was only twenty-three he declared that 'dans la
première période de la vie d'artiste il est mieux de jeter
du dehors tout ce qu'on a de vraiment intime, d'original,
d'individuel'. It sounds rather forbiddingly professional
for twenty-three, and in fact Flaubert had a fling on
St. Antony before sitting down to *Madame Bovary*, his
first real exercise in his self-imposed discipline. It was
much more than an exercise, of course, for Flaubert had
a passion of indignation that needed vent; but without
his resolve to be impersonal it would have wasted itself
in vain.

In sacrificing his personality Flaubert thought he
sacrificed much. He believed that he was 'born lyrical'.
Born romantic would have been nearer the truth, for
we have to qualify lyrical by his repeated and truthful
confession that his talent was not 'primesautier'. His
natural bent was towards romantic dream and romantic
tirade, and his gift of lyrical expression very small. But
the strength of a desire cannot be measured by the
capacity of satisfying it, and there is no cause to doubt
Flaubert's sincerity when he rebelled, as he rebelled
continually, against the 'ugliness' of his work on *Madame*

Bovary. Ah, what he would do when he had a subject of his own! He was tired, tired to death of the bourgeois. It was time to drop them for ever. But the subject of his own never came. At first he imagined that *La Tentation* and *Salammbô* were completely congenial, but the illusion was brief; and though he never went so far as to declare that these subjects were ugly, his complaints and his torments were the same. It was not surprising that in his last two books he should return to the detested bourgeois. In one sense at least all subjects were the same to him; he suffered equally from them all.

Two demons stood always between Flaubert and his dreams—the demon of style and the demon of truthfulness. Of the two it was the demon of truthfulness that tormented him the more. It drove him to fantastic efforts of documentation; his researches for *Salammbô* were prodigious, and at the very commencement of *Bouvard et Pécuchet* he confessed that he had read 1,500 volumes for it. Yet he seems never to have asked himself jesting Pilate's question. What was this truth for which he laboured? Had he asked, he would have been forced to reply; the truth of history, not of art. But he was never able to disentangle them. His letters sometimes make nightmare reading. He must find an actual piece of France for Bouvard and Pécuchet to farm in. It was not enough to invent the episode of their geological expedition to the coast; young de Maupassant must provide him with a stretch of real cliff where the complicated event was possible: and he wrote again and again till he got it. A passion for truth of this kind is a purely morbid condition in a writer; he must indeed be 'drunk with ink' to feel it. Such truth has no value in itself, and the search for it is bound to prejudice the truth which is proper to literature. The verisimilitude of art does not depend on documents—neither indeed does the verisimilitude of history—but upon the creative imagination and the sensibility from which the imagination is replenished. In both these Flaubert was deficient; the range of his sensibility was not large, nor his creative imagination robust. He tried to eke them out with a reference library, with the result that in all his books, save *Madame Bovary* and *Un Cœur Simple*, his tenuous characters dissolve away into their own background.

With the demon of style, as he understood style, his struggle was more successful. But in order to appraise his victory we must remember how he understood it. So many passages in his letters reveal his conception that the choice is embarrassing; one may suffice:

'Ce qui distingue les grands génies c'est la généralisation et la création; ils résument en un type des personnalités éparses et apportent à la conscience du genre humain des personnages nouveaux; est-ce qu'on ne croit pas à l'existence de Don Quichotte comme à celle de César? Shakespeare est quelque chose de formidable sous ce rapport: ce n'était pas un homme, mais un continent; il y avait de grands hommes en lui, des foules entières, des paysages; ils n'ont pas besoin de faire du style, ceux-là, ils sont forts en dépit de toutes les fautes et à cause d'elles; mais nous, les petits, nous ne valons que par l'exécution achevée. Hugo en ce siècle enfoncera tout le monde quoiqu'il soit plein de mauvaises choses, mais quel souffle! Je hasarde ici une proposition que je n'oserais dire nulle part: c'est que les très grands hommes écrivent souvent fort mal, et tant mieux pour eux.'

A style of which the greatest writers have no need, to the want of which they owe their greatness, is a dubious light to follow. It was less dangerous for Flaubert, who saw his own limitations clearly, than for

those who have blindly followed him. But probably
Flaubert also paid a price for his obsession; probably it
distracted his attention from the content of his work
and induced him to spend energies that might have gone
to the expansion of his sensibility upon the painful
polishing of a hollow surface; the substance which could
have made it solid his starved sensibility could not
provide. One dare not dogmatize. Who knows for
certain that a writer by taking thought can add a cubit
to the stature of his soul? Possibly Flaubert, being the
man he was, made a right choice; possibly he persevered
where he could make some progress and abandoned the
road along which advance was barred. But the probability and the evidence point the other way. The book
whose style he laboured least—a Flaubertian minimum
is not as other men's—is the one by which he is chiefly
remembered. The youthful *Madame Bovary* has a validity
which he was to achieve only once again, in *Un Cœur
Simple*. *Madame Bovary* alone answers to his own definition of a great work of literature; it gathers scattered
personalities into a type and brings new personalities to
the consciousness of the human race. Emma Bovary
and Monsieur Homais are figures of this kind; they are
(except perhaps Félicie) the only ones in Flaubert's
work.

Flaubert began his career with what is, take it all in
all, a masterpiece; he was to write no other. *L'Éducation
Sentimentale* is not one. It may be life, but it is not living;
it is a work of history rather than literature. Flaubert
had no certain hold of his characters, and his handling
of his theme at the crucial moment falls to the level of
melodrama. The most famous passage in the book is
the death of Dussardier:

'Mais, sur les marches de Tortoni, un homme—Dussardier—remarquable de loin à sa haute taille, restait sans plus bouger qu'une cariatide.

Un des agents qui marchait en tête, le tricorne sur les yeux, le menaça de son épée.

L'autre alors, s'avançant d'un pas, se mit à crier,—

— "Vive la République!"

Il tomba sur le dos, les bras en croix.

Un hurlement d'horreur s'éleva de la foule. L'agent fit un cercle autour de lui avec son regard; et Frédéric, béant, reconnut Sénécal.

Il voyagea.

Il connut la mélancolie des paquebots, les froids réveils sous la tente, l'étourdissement des paysages et des ruines, l'amertume des sympathies interrompues.

Il revint.'

'Et Frédéric, béant, reconnut Sénécal,' has been for years the object of an esoteric admiration as a master-piece of style. In a different book it might, indeed, have been overwhelming; in the gray monotone of *L'Éducation Sentimentale* it is a splash of discordant red. The dramatic artifice tears through the even texture of the narrative: it belongs to another world of seeing and feeling, and the measure of its discordance is our astonishment at Sénécal's surprising change. If a respectable solicitor were to slip behind a screen and reappear in a cardboard nose and a pair of huge moustaches, it could not be more disturbing than this *coup de théâtre* in the most laboriously realistic story ever written.

Only if style could be separated from content, the surface from the perceptions which make it solid, could Flaubert's style be praised without reserve. The distinction, as he knew, cannot be made. And Flaubert's style is sometimes perfect, sometimes bad, more often in-different than either. It is at its highest level in *Un Cœur*

Simple. There it follows the contour of his thought with a perfect economy.

'Elle se levait dès l'aube, pour ne pas manquer la messe, et travaillait jusqu'au soir sans interruption; puis, le dîner étant fini, la vaisselle en ordre et la porte bien close, elle enfouissait la bûche sous les cendres et s'endormait devant l'âtre, son rosaire à la main. Personne, dans les marchandages, ne montrait plus d'entêtement. Quant à la propreté, le poli de ses casseroles faisait le désespoir des autres servantes. Économe, elle mangeait avec lenteur, et recueillait du doigt sur la table les miettes de son pain—un pain de douze livres, cuit exprès pour elle, et qui durait vingt jours.

En toute saison elle portait un mouchoir d'indienne fixé dans le dos par une épingle, un bonnet lui cachant ses cheveux, des bas gris, un jupon rouge, et par-dessus sa camisole un tablier à bavette, comme les infirmières d'hôpital.

Son visage était maigre et sa voix aiguë. A vingt-cinq ans, on lui en donnait quarante. Dès la cinquantaine, elle ne marqua plus aucun âge; — et, toujours silencieuse, la taille droite, et les gestes mesurés, semblait une femme de bois, fonctionnant d'une manière automatique.

Elle avait eu, comme une autre, son histoire d'amour.'

How exquisite—to descend to particulars—is the order of the words in 'recueillait du doigt sur la table les miettes de son pain'; it gives the gesture its significance and yields to the rhythm of the paragraph. And the final sentence, which opens the second chapter, is characteristic of Flaubert at his best. He was a master of the short sentences even more than the period. The effects he wrung from it are sometimes astonishing. Here the contrast between the movement which ends 'une femme de bois fonctionnant d'une manière automatique' and the short sentence which follows is carefully modulated by the insertion of 'comme une autre' where we should not expect it. It not only gives us the very substance of Félicie, but saturates the narrative with a sense of time.

This power of awakening in us a sense of the process of time was Flaubert's most individual achievement as a writer. We might also say that wherever we are struck with the apparently inexplicable beauty of a page or a passage in his work we shall find the secret of the enchantment in this presentation of time. *Un Cœur Simple* unrolls a life from beginning to end in ninety short pages, and we feel every year of it drop slowly into the past. In the passage we have quoted from *L'Éducation Sentimentale* the significance of 'Il voyagea' is unmistakable, and there again Flaubert uses the division of a chapter to achieve his effect. His devices are innumerable. In the last sentence of *Hérodias* it is the choice and placing of an adverb. 'Comme elle (the head of Jokanaan) était très lourde, ils la portaient alternativement.' There it is too deliberate. But the first twenty pages of *Madame Bovary* are a splendid example of Flaubert's resource. The story is swift and unhesitating up to the eighteenth page. Charles Bovary's schooldays and the events of his first marriage flow by in a steady stream; it is one life among many. Suddenly the tempo is changed in a paragraph. Emma Rouault has appeared.

'Elle le reconduisait toujours jusqu'à la première marche du perron. Lorsqu' on n'avait pas encore amené son cheval, elle restait là. On s'était dit adieu, on ne se parlait plus; le grand air l'entourait, levant pêle-mêle les petits cheveux follets de sa nuque, ou secouant sur sa hanche les cordons de son tablier qui se tortillaient comme des banderolles. Une fois, par un temps de dégel, l'écorce des arbres suintait dans la cour, la neige sur les couvertures des bâtiments se fondait. Elle était sur le seuil; elle alla chercher son ombrelle, elle l'ouvrit. L'ombrelle, de soie gorge-de-pigeon, que traversait le soleil, éclairait de reflets mobiles la peau blanche de sa figure. Elle souriait là-dessous à la chaleur tiède; et on entendait les gouttes d'eau, une à une, tomber sur la moire tendue.'

It is like a sudden oasis of calm in which everything can be seen, everything heard. The languorous beauty of the last sentence echoes on like the sounds of the drops it registers. We feel that that day was the first in his life for Charles Bovary.

If one were to press home the analysis of those characteristic effects of Flaubert, they would be found to depend generally on two elements, an unusual use of the verb tenses which an English reader can more easily feel than describe, and the manipulation of the rhythm. A period like this from *Madame Bovary* has the complicated rhythm of a fine piece of blank verse. Flaubert learnt something of this from Chateaubriand, and another part from Voltaire and Montesquieu, from whom he quoted with delight: 'Les vices d'Alexandre étaient extrêmes comme ses vertus; il était terrible dans sa colère; elle le rendait cruel.' A thousand sentences after that pattern can be found in his work. The quality that fascinated him in it was not so much the rhythm as the close texture on which the larger effects of rhythm depend. Each one of those pronouns helps to bind the parts of the sentence into one inseparable whole. Flaubert, as always, turned his admirations to account. He worked upon the hints they gave him indefatigably, and he fashioned for himself an instrument upon which no tones were impossible.

Because of this Flaubert is indeed a great master; but

not of the greatest. In the years he spent on perfecting the instrument he forgot, if he ever knew, what tunes are most worth playing; and too often in his work we hear him sounding idly for their own intrinsic beauty notes which have no part in any larger plan. He was never passionately possessed by a comprehensive theme, and he never clearly saw that the rendering of such a theme was the final purpose of all the explorations of language on which he lavished himself. His sacrifice was as pathetic as it was noble. When we read such a passage as this in his letters—and there are many of them—we feel as sad as he.

'Néanmoins, il y a une chose triste, c'est de voir combien de grands hommes arrivent aisément à l'effet en dehors de l'art même: quoi de plus mal bâti que bien des choses de Rabelais, Cervantes, Molière, et Hugo? Mais quels coups de poing subits? Quelle puissance dans un seul mot! Nous, il faut entasser l'un sur l'autre un tas de petits cailloux pour faire nos pyramides qui ne vont pas à la centième partie des leurs, lesquelles sont d'un seul bloc.'

What is this 'Art' which the masters triumph by ignoring? If they have no 'Art' what is the value of 'Art' at all? And why call it 'Art'? Flaubert never answered the question: the greatest writers remained prodigies for him; there was no room for them in his philosophy.

But for Flaubert, though they existed on heights unapproachable, they did exist, and he never forgot them. What are we to say of a generation that has seen in Flaubert's 'Art' the highest achievement of literature, and in Flaubert himself the perfect type of the great writer? Were it not the fact, the collective hallucination would appear like a chapter in a fairy tale. We can see the cause of the aberration. Flaubert's 'Art' is an art which minor writers can understand; in pretending to surrender themselves to it—for the patient labour of a real surrender is much too painful—they have the satisfaction of manipulating a mystery. But the mystification has lasted too long. The invention of 'Art' has done no good to art, and it has interposed a veil between Flaubert's work and the general judgement. To be critical of Flaubert is to prejudice a vested interest, so large an edifice has been built upon the insecure foundation.

Flaubert came as near to the highest literary genius as a man can come by the taking of pains. Just as his example will be a perpetual encouragement to all honest craftsmen of literature, it will be a will o' the wisp to those who presume to measure the giants by it. Flaubert's work can never cease to smell of the lamp, but by the writing of one fine book and one perfect story, and his devoted researches into the capacity of language, he is one of the greatest heroes in the second rank of letters. More than this, his correspondence shows him to us as one of the most lovable of all writers, for though we smile at him tearing his hair in the silence of his study, our smile is the smile of sympathy and admiration. But those who claim more for him than this would lose all, if it were possible, for they can exalt him only by deposing greater men than he. Flaubert stands in no need of such extravagant admiration, and we know him well enough to be certain that he would have resented bitterly a worship paid to himself at the cost of divinities he adored. [OCTOBER 1921.

XIII

STENDHAL

No one has better described the impression made by
Stendhal than Goethe, who wrote in 1818: 'Er zieht
an, er stosst ab, interessiert und ärgert, und so kann man
ihn nicht loswerden.' ('He attracts, repels, interests,
irritates, and one can't get away from him.') That was
written after reading *Rome, Naples, and Florence,* which
M. Édouard Champion has lately republished in his
superb edition of the complete works, and the description fits the particular book perhaps a little more exactly
than any of the others. It so obviously ought to be a dull
work, and it so obviously is not. It has neither system
nor shape; it is concerned with a society that has passed
out of mind; it is studded with the irrelevant, tangential
speculations of a perpetually curious mind, with odd
facts of history, with long and enthusiastic appreciations
of forgotten Italian operas and unremembered singers.
Yet we are held. Stendhal's facts are not like anybody
else's facts. They are like objects looked at from a
peculiar and unexpected angle. We only half recognize
them. The proportions are queer. At first they are
almost silly, then they become bizarre, then fascinating,
and then—at least for a period in most literary lives—
all-absorbing.

Stendhal was a man of many surfaces. There are bold
men who call themselves *stendhaliens* and profess to be
adept in *le beylisme*; but they are not to be trusted. It is
true that Stendhal had an attitude to life, a philosophy
of conduct, that might be imitated. But the man who
actively followed Beyle's precepts would, by the mere
fact, be very different from Beyle. For this seeming

rusé realist was the embodiment of timidity; this amateur
of the *amour-passion* was one of the most backward
love-makers who ever existed. In M. Arbelet's most
admirable biography, *La Jeunesse de Stendhal*, which is
published as part (and a worthy part) of the collected
edition, you may read of the comedy or the tragedy of
young Beyle's initiation into love at Milan. It is an
unfamiliar but characteristic episode in the man's life,
which was stained through and through as it were with
a dye of some paradoxical uniqueness. One feels that
he was born in a momentary interregnum of the *Zeitgeist,*
just as in the actual world he happened to be educated
in one of those strange schools which were the immediate
product of the Revolution, where masters and pupils
alike were fired by a passion for *la Raison*—schools which
lasted barely three years, just long enough to give a
unique impress to the one boy with a touch of genius
who might, on merely statistical grounds, be expected
to be born in the period.

If one were writing the book upon Beyle which has
still to be written—it will be the work of an English
critic, for no Frenchman could have sufficient detachment, or even sufficient understanding—one would begin
by showing how a cornucopia of uniquenesses was
made ready to be emptied upon the head of the infant
Henri Beyle. M. Arbelet has gathered most of the
material for a study of his astonishing parents and
relations, those bourgeois aristocrats (like the Rênals
of *Le Rouge et le Noir*) who were so much more exclusive
even than the *grands bourgeois* of modern France. When
one comes to know them a little more closely, to see
them a little more clearly, than is possible through the
melodramatic kaleidoscope of *La Vie de Henri Brulard*
one comes to look upon Beyle as a kind of infant Samuel

dedicated to one knows not what deity of contrariety
and paradox. One feels, rather than understands, the
reason of the inevitability which imposes itself upon any
one who attempts even in the scope of a brief essay to
define the substance of Beyle, the man and the writer.
Every comparison is turned ineluctably into paradox.
The outward garment of his style suggests the influence
of Voltaire; in fact, Beyle hated Voltaire, and the real
influence was much rather Jean-Jacques. His whole
manner is that of an aristocrat of aristocrats; he was, in
fact, and most profoundly, a republican, a libertarian,
and a radical. Most sincerely in the literary contro-
versy of his age Beyle insisted that he was a romantic;
in fact, he detested Chateaubriand, and he was pretty
exactly what we call a realist. His lucid and exact
psychological analysis recalls no one in the French
tradition so directly as Racine; in fact, Beyle could not
abide Racine, and most honestly and for the most substantial reasons idolized Shakespeare. 'Adorava Shakespeare' was the alternative epitaph to the one which
he finally chose: 'Arrigo Beyle Milanese: vissè, scrissè,
amò.' The art of Shakespeare and the life of Italy—
between Rivoli and the Risorgimento, be it understood—
may fairly be said to have been the two passions whose
rule over him endured throughout his life.

Beyle is, perhaps, the smallest of great men; but he is
also one of the most compact, and his title to be called
great is proved not least by the wholly peculiar persist-
ence with which he seems to avoid all classification.
He makes a queer final impression—how delighted he
would have been to read it!—as of a miniature, desiccated Shakespeare, and, indeed, one can easily conceive
a definition of him in terms which in a richer, riper
world of perceptions would apply to Shakespeare. His

universe of men was also blank between the aristocrat and the peasant, and it may be for the same reason. He confesses that because he was a bourgeois, the bourgeois had become as intolerable to him as the taste of oysters to a man who has had a surfeit of them; he had supped too full of the horrors of the bourgeoisie in childhood ever to contemplate them again. The middle class were ciphers in his system of values, and even an ideal member of it remained a cipher, just as zero, raised to the nth power, remains zero. 'Ce qui est exactement raisonnable ne donne pas prise aux beaux-arts; j'estime un sage républicain des États-Unis, mais je l'oublie à tout jamais en quelques jours: ce n'est pas un homme pour moi, c'est une chose.' Therefore, although he was by impulse a realist, he was nevertheless a romantic because he had a theory of reality. Not all that existed in the shape of human beings was real to him. This anti-bourgeois speck in his telescope, he wrote in *Henri Brulard*, had been very useful to him with the characters of his novels. It was true; but the word 'bourgeois' had by that time come to denote for him not so much a social class as a type of being. The reality of a man for Stendhal lay in his faculty of allowing all that is prudential and calculating in him to be dominated by what is instinctive and passionate.

That is a fairly complete and coherent attitude towards life; it certainly has its counterpart in Shakespeare; it is, moreover, what we might call a very good working basis for a literary artist. But it does not in the least resemble that enlightened hedonism which the 'Beylistes' profess to find in their idol. Beyle, indeed, makes a poor showing as a hedonist. The overwhelming impulses of soul which he set highest, and counted most real among human capacities, the precious *élans d'âme,* were likely to prove annihilating to their vehicles. Indeed, they not only annihilated his heroes and heroines, Fabrice, Julien Sorel, Mademoiselle de la Môle, Clélia, and the rest, but they came near to being his own undoing at one or two points of his own career. To be interesting to Beyle people must be ready to surrender their lives at the summons of a *grande passion*; to be interesting to himself he had to believe that the same readiness lay in him. It is therefore inexact to call him a romantic, even though he called himself one. Your true romantic is ready to surrender himself only to dreams; his *élan d'âme* has little or no repercussion in the visible world. The real world is altogether too sordid, and perhaps too difficult a place for him to be concerned with it. His passions are veritably passive. It was, however, the essence of Stendhal's conception of passion that it should issue, and issue immediately in act. Whether the act seems grandiose or ridiculous, momentous or merely bizarre, was of small account; it was precisely indifferent. He prefaces almost every one of his stories of *la vie passionelle* in *Rome, Naples et Florence* with the warning that it will seem ridiculous, but the implication behind the warning is that if you find it ridiculous, you are a poor creature. The faculty which he admired in men had two complementary aspects. Looked at from the inside it was passion, the *élan d'âme*; from the outside it was energy, *la force*. This is the meaning of his paradox: 'J'aime la force, et de la force que j'aime, une fourmi peut en montrer autant qu'un éléphant.'

Stendhal's attitude to life was not romantic, therefore; it was tragic. It falls in between the classical and the romantic attitudes. His ideal is neither the harmonious man of the Greeks nor the gesticulating, dreaming hero of romanticism; it is, really, the hero of a Shakespearean tragedy, a hero who plays his part in the active life of a real world. In order to give literary expression to this tragic hero-worship, Stendhal had to become what is generally called a realist. But just as the term 'romantic' has to be given an unfamiliar and improper meaning to fit him, 'realist' has also to be given a precise and particular sense. Realist in the proper critical meaning he was not. A good deal more than half human life was supremely uninteresting to him. But the part he was interested in had a sort of super-reality to compensate. The problem was how to convey and communicate this, how (in the expressive phrase of the working artist) 'to get it across'. An unobtrusive sentence in *Rome, Naples et Florence*—we are endeavouring to explain Stendhal on the evidence of this single book—gives us his solution. 'On n'a jamais du feu,' he writes, 'qu'en écrivant la langue qu'on parle à sa maîtresse et à ses rivaux.'

Now there is much more in Stendhal's style than is indicated here; but that dictum contains the solid basis of some of his most remarkable achievements—passionate episodes expressed in the natural language of passion. On the creative side one can think immediately of a dozen passages in the two great novels where the theory is superbly exemplified—for instance, the 'Qu'avez-vous dans la poche de côté de votre habit?' of Mathilde de la Môle—on the critical, it is a main count in his one-sided, but convincing case against Scott. 'Ses personnages passionnés semblent avoir honte d'eux-mêmes'; therefore they are unreal. This principle is the chief of the two tendencies that unite to form Stendhal's 'realism'. From his childhood upwards he was, in regard to literature, a dissatisfied rather than a disillusioned romantic.

M. Arbelet has unearthed a singularly interesting passage from one of his unpublished notes which bears upon this. It was written before he was twenty:

'Dans les romans on ne nous offre qu'une nature choisie; nous nous formons nos types de bonheur d'après les romans. Parvenus à l'âge où nous devons être heureux . . . nous nous étonnons de deux choses: la première, de ne pas éprouver du tout les sentiments auxquels nous nous attendions; la deuxième, si nous les éprouvons, de ne pas les sentir comme ils sont peints dans les romans.'

Two years later he re-read his note, and added: 'Voilà l'histoire de ma vie; mon roman était les ouvrages de Rousseau.' Stendhal himself was destined to offer to future generations a *nature choisie*, more sedulously selected, perhaps, than that of any other considerable novelist. It was not the ignoring of half reality that shocked him, but being unreal in the expression of the reality you chose. Because he was consistently and profoundly a 'romantic', he hated with a threefold hatred romantic falseness and pomposity; because he really had a tragic attitude to life, the high falutin' of French classical tragedy goaded him to a frenzy. It was making his heartfelt realities ridiculous. From this he directly derived his detestation of the phrase and the circumlocution, which remained with him all his life, and his at first sight strange desire, which lasted to middle age, to write a good comedy. An instinct told him that the drama was the most perfect vehicle for his tragic view of life; another instinct told him that a genre in which you had to write *coursier* for *cheval* and the precious word *pistolet* was taboo, was intolerable. To get natural speech on to the stage, he must write comedy. It may seem a fantastic conclusion; fantastic it must seem if you have read the outline of any of his projected 'comedies'—irrefutable evidence that he had not a shred of a sense of humour—but yet inevitable.

The other component of his style, a bare and vigorous clarity of analytical exposition, came from two sources. He was, as we have said, a devout believer in the tragic attitude. Tragic heroes were real people; he had met plenty of them in the Italian society he loved. He wanted to prove that they existed, to take them to pieces, as it were, in the intervals when they were not expressing *élans d'âme* in the natural language of passion. Here the ideologists who had been triumphant in the French educational system for the three brief and impressionable years he spent at the École Centrale at Grenoble lent him powerful aid. Those forgotten psychologists, Destutt de Tracy and Condillac, whose names recur so often in his pages, were indeed his masters of method here. Hence came the passion for *la lo-gique* which in his curious drawl he so often impressed upon Mérimée, and his recourse to the Code Napoléon as a model of descriptive style. His education and the demands of his theory of life and art worked together for good. His heroes, being heroes of action, were saved from perishing in a maze of super-subtle psychology; since their supreme moments had to be expressed in the natural language of passion, they were also saved (with all due deference to weighty, but nevertheless heretic opinion) from becoming 'desiccated'.

Stendhal, in brief, was a tragic realist. Tragic realism is, on the whole, an unusual kind; but some of the greatest works of literary art belong to it, the *Medea* and *Antony and Cleopatra*, *Anna Karenina*, and *The Possessed*. Stendhal differs from the writers called up by these names in that he held his faith a perceptible shade more naïvely than they. It was for him not merely the attitude of an artist towards life, not merely a philosophy which enabled the artist to express his vision of the truth and quality of life, it was also, and perhaps chiefly, a philosophy of conduct. Tragic heroes did not merely exist because their destiny was forced upon them; it was man's duty to be one. The first thing was to be *une âme supérieure* (his beloved phrase), the second to assert it in act, the third—and a bad third—was to write about it. And here is the reason why, although there is no real incongruity in naming Stendhal with Euripides and Shakespeare and Tolstoy and Dostoevsky, a vital difference remains. To a casual glance it presents itself as a constant amateurishness in Stendhal the artist. We must look deeper than that, however; and, looking deeper, we shall discover it to be a profound naïvety. What satisfies only a part of the great writer's mind satisfied the whole of his: in other words, Stendhal was even less a creator of heroes than a hero-worshipper.

[SEPTEMBER 1920.

XIV

A CRITICAL CREDO

IT is a waste and weary labour to open up again the old question of reviewing and criticism. On the one hand, there should be no distinction between them; the reviewer's business is to criticize the book before him. But too often in practice the reviewer is expected to compile a library list for the average unintelligent reader. On the other hand, economic necessity nowadays compels the critic to become a reviewer. So that the valuable modern distinction is not so much the distinction between the critic and the reviewer, as the impossibilists frequently urge, as that between the critic-reviewer and the puff-reviewer. We must leave out the puff-reviewer. God will reward him as surely as his employer does.

Speaking of criticism, Remy de Gourmont said that 'the whole effort of a sincere man is to erect his personal impressions into laws'. That is the motto of a true criticism, conscious of its limitations and its strength. The emphasis falls even more decidedly upon the law-making than upon the personal basis of the impressions, for that is inevitable. The man who is content to record his own impressions, without making an effort to stabilize them in the form of laws, whatever he is, is not a critic. A law or rule, or rather a system of laws or rules, is necessary to the critic; it is a record of all his past impressions and reactions; but it must be his own law, his own system, refined by his own effort out of his own experience. Otherwise he is a pedant and not a critic.

The function of criticism is, therefore, primarily the function of literature itself, to provide a means of self-expression for the critic. He begins like any other writer, with the conviction (which may of course be an illusion) that his views and conclusions on the subject-matter which is literature are of importance in themselves and to others; and he proceeds to promulgate and propagate them. Like any other writer, he stands or falls in the long run, by the closer or more remote approximation of his views to the common experience of that comparatively small fraction of the human race which itself comes to conclusions about life and literature, which is the concentrated record of life. As Dr. Johnson said:

'Nothing can please many and please long, but just representations of human nature. Particular manners can be known to few, and therefore few only can judge how nearly they are copied. The irregular combinations of fanciful invention may delight awhile, by that novelty of which the common satiety of life sends us all in quest; but the pleasures of sudden wonder are soon exhausted, and the mind can repose only on the stability of truth.'

The critic stands or falls by the stability of his truth, and necessarily by his skill in communicating his truth.

That the critic has to interest his readers is true, but in exactly the same sense as it is true that every writer has to interest his readers. He does not have to aim at being more interesting than other writers. This is one of the prime heresies of modern criticism. Its adherents appear to hold that a critical article is a kind of knock-about turn. Unless the critic is turning a somersault or making a grimace in every sentence, he is dull. Another and more persuasive heresy is that it is the critic's business to make the best of a bad book by picking out the one or two plums that have wandered into the wilderness of dough. A critic, argue its adherents, has to communicate 'gusto' to his readers, no matter what book he may be writing about. These seem to me to be pure heresies, and the critics who embrace them will surely be forgotten.

Criticism is a particular art of literature. It is possible not to like the art, and possible for the critic to regret that his art is not liked. But it is not, or ought not to be possible for a critic to play the traitor to his art in order to get a bigger audience for his raree-show. Because a sculptor knows that sculpture is not popular, he does not paint moustaches on his figures or plant billycock hats on the top of their heads. The critic's business is to express himself by expressing his opinion on the work of literature before him. He has therefore to make sure that his opinion is his true opinion; he has to safeguard himself against accidental and temporary disturbances of his sensibility. Hence the need for a system of principles, refined out of his more constant reactions, to control momentary enthusiasms and passing disgusts.

Moreover, he is concerned to elucidate the significance of the work before him, for his verdict is a verdict as to significance. A work of literature may possess significance of various kinds; it may have historical, ethical, or aesthetic significance; that is, it may have importance at a particular phase of the human consciousness, or it may be valuable as expressing a particular attitude towards human life, or it may have more or less of a certain kind of artistic perfection which compels a peculiar artistic emotion in the reader. A work may have significance of one of these kinds, or all of them, or any combination of them. A critic is bound to have a predisposition towards one of these kinds of significance; he will be predominantly an historian, like Sainte-

Beuve, a moralist like Matthew Arnold, or a technician like Dr. Bridges. He ought to be aware of his predisposition and alert to prevent it from running away with him. A perfect critic would combine all these predispositions in equal parts, but perfect critics are at least as rare as perfect writers. It is as much as one can ask that a critic should try to correct his predisposition by training his appreciation of other kinds.

Once criticism is accepted as an independent literary art there need be no heart-searching among critics because they have so little practical influence on the sale of books. That is the fact in England at any rate. It is a hundred times more profitable to an author for the *Daily Mail* to declare 'This book will be a success' than for the best critic on *The Times Literary Supplement* to give exact and convincing reasons why the book ought to be a success. Critical articles and essays are read for themselves; at their best they are perfectly self-contained; they do not demand that the reader should dash out and purchase the books which they discuss, and as often as not they are read with the greatest interest by those who are already themselves profoundly familiar with the subject.

Putting a valuation upon new books is perhaps the least valuable, as it is certainly the most dangerous, part of criticism. It is almost impossible for a literary critic to be really sincere in dealing with contemporary production. It is as difficult for him to tell the truth about the bad work of men who have done good, as to tell the truth about the good work of men who have done bad. In the first case his hand is checked by fear of doing harm, in the second by the fear of doing good. Again, it is intolerable to be severe to a well-meaning beginner, although a critic knows that the road to hell is paved with good intentions. There are too many thorns in the path of criticism of contemporaries. For we have not even mentioned the personal resentment too often cherished by our victims. The dangers of log-rolling are at least equalled by the dangers of revenge. A successful author, however much he may be dubious of the genuineness of his own powers, cannot help believing that his success is somehow due to his merits; he is bound to persuade himself that a slating is the expression of some personal hostility.

Unfortunately, few critics are in the happy position of being able to write about contemporaries only when they can sincerely praise them. For the most part they have to conform to the exigencies of reviewing, to write on texts they could not choose, to consider susceptibilities that are an obstacle to their free expression. No doubt the English tradition of anonymity is a defence against some of these evils. But it leaves the door open to other worse ones. A critic does not care to hide behind an editorial 'we' when he attacks a writer; nor on the other hand is it good to be compelled always to hide one's light under a bushel. A good criticism is as much a work of art as a good poem; its author deserves his reward in reputation as well as money. Besides, if his readers are not permitted to distinguish his work they cannot follow the sequence and evolution of his ideas. A critic cannot be always enunciating his principles. What looks like the veriest dogmatism in an isolated review may, if put into relation to other utterances, be seen to have a convincing scheme of values behind it.

Criticism is an art. It has its own technique. Ideally, at least, this technique would have its different perfection for each several critic. But we may outline so much of the method as seems to be essential to the most important kind of criticism, appreciation.

First, the critic should endeavour to convey the whole effect of the work he is criticizing, its peculiar uniqueness. Second, to work back and define the unique quality of the sensibility which necessitated this expression. Third, to establish the determining causes of this sensibility. (Here the relevant circumstances of the writer's life have their proper place.) Fourth, to analyse the means by which this sensibility was given expression; in other words, to conduct a technical examination into the style. Fifth, a still closer examination of a perfectly characteristic passage, that is, a passage in which the author's sensibility is completely expressed. This fifth and final movement is really a return to the first, but with the important difference that the relevant material has been ordered and placed before the reader.

The various phases in this symphonic movement of an ideal criticism may, of course, be ordered quite differently. The historical or the ethical critic will enlarge more on the nature of the sensibility, its value in itself and its relation to other types of sensibility; he will pay little or no attention to the means by which this sensibility is expressed. He will not be a worse critic for that, but he will be a less *literary* critic. On the other hand, the critic who is unable to adjudicate between the values of various kinds of sensibility has no means of distinguishing between great art and perfect art. That judgement is essential to a true criticism, in spite of (or rather in virtue of) the fact that it is in the last resort an ethical judgement.

There is not much need to worry ourselves about the function of criticism any more than we worry about the function of poetry. Both are arts; both have to give delight; both have to give the delights which are proper to themselves as arts. If it gives this delight criticism is creative, for it enables the reader to discover beauties and significances which he had not seen, or to see those which he had himself inglimpsed in a new and revealing light. What, I think, we may reasonably ask, is that criticism should be less timid; that it should openly accept the fact that its deepest judgements are moral. A critic should be conscious of his moral assumptions and take pains to put into them the highest morality of which he is capable. That is only another way of saying that the critic should be conscious of himself as an artist. He should be aware of the responsibilities imposed by his art; he should respect the technique of his craft. He should not be cheap, he should not be shallow, he should not be insincere, either in praise or blame, but above all, in these modern times, he should not be insincere in praise. [SEPTEMBER 1921.

NOTES

Page 4. This theory, which I still regard as probable, tends to fix the actual date of the catastrophe in Shakespeare's affair with the Dark Lady at about 1598, because two of the most embittered of the Dark Lady sonnets (138 and 144) were published, piratically, by Jaggard in *The Passionate Pilgrim* in 1599. I should imagine from their position at the head of the volume that they were regarded by the pirate as the scandalous tit-bits of his 'anthology'. The Quarto of *Love's Labour's Lost*, which contains manifest, but not yet embittered, references to the Dark Lady, was published in 1598. According to the title-page, it was 'newly corrected and augmented', and the traces of correction and expansion are evident in the text. Further, the title-page says: 'As it was presented before her Highness this last Christmas', i.e. Christmas, 1597. 1598, therefore, seems to be indicated as the year of the trouble. The curious should read Mr. Arthur Acheson's extremely ingenious volume *Shakespeare's Sonnet Story, 1592–1598*. It is too elaborate to be wholly convincing; but a residue of probability remains.

Page 26. Now, ten years later, I feel that I was guilty of super-subtlety in this passage. Nevertheless, I leave it as it stood.

Page 54. In a letter Mr. H. O. White, of Sheffield University, corrects my statement: 'We must suppose that the *Dirge for Cymbeline*, first printed in 1749, was one of his last poems, if not the very last.' The Dirge, says Mr. White, first appeared in 1744, in the second and revised edition of the *Epistle to Sir Thomas Hanmer*; while the version which appeared in 1749, in *The Gentleman's Magazine*, was garbled. The point of bibliography, in the case of a poet of such little output as Collins, is of unusual importance; and since the same mistake is made in the two most authoritative English editions of Collins's works, Mr. White's correction needs to be put on record. I do not think, however, that the alteration materially affects the argument of the essay.

Page 61. Professor Garrod in his valuable book on Collins points out many of these obscurities, of some of which I was unaware. But I think that sometimes he bears a little too hard on Collins, as in his criticism of lines 4–8 of the *Ode to Evening*. Very little of Shakespeare's imagery would stand the strain of such analysis.

Page 64. It has been pointed out to me by Mr. Bruce Richmond

that the well-known stanza of the *Elegy in a Country Churchyard*
contains a reminiscence of Lucretius's beautiful lines:

> Jam jam non domus accipiet te laeta, neque uxor
> Optima, nec dulces occurrent oscula nati
> Praeripere. . . .

It had not occurred to me; but once suggested the reminiscence
is self-evident. The question may also arise whether Thomson,
Collins, and Gray had not all of them the same Lucretian original
in mind. But the phraseology of Thomson and Collins is against
this. I imagine that Thomson's lines were an independent and
original imagination, and that Collins consciously imitated them,
while Gray had both Thomson and Lucretius in mind. The
reduplication of 'in vain' is conclusive for Collins's imitation, while
'the blazing hearth' does not leave much doubt that Gray was
thinking of Thomson as well as Lucretius.

Page 88. I cannot help thinking how strangely different would
have been William Blake's answer to this same question of Mr. de
la Mare.

> But others of the Sons of Los build Moments & Minutes &
> Hours,
> And Days & Months & Years, & Ages & Periods, wondrous
> buildings!
> And every Moment has a Couch of gold for soft repose,
> (A Moment equals a pulsation of the artery)
> And between every two Moments stands a Daughter of Beulah
> To feed the Sleepers on their Couches with maternal care.
> And every Minute has an azure Tent with silken Veils;
> And every Hour has a bright golden Gate carvèd with skill;
> And every Day & Night has walls of brass & Gates of
> adamant,
> Shining like precious Stones & ornamented with appropriate
> signs:
> And every Month a silver pavèd Terrace builded high;
> And every Year invulnerable Barriers with high Towers;
> And every Age is Moated deep, with Bridges of silver & gold;
> And every Seven Ages is Incirclèd with a Flaming Fire.
> Now Seven Ages is amounting to Two Hundred Years.
> Each has its Guard, each Moment, Minute, Hour, Day, Month
> & Year:
> All are the work of Fairy hands of the Four Elements:
> The Guard are Angels of Providence on duty evermore.

Every Time less than a pulsation of the artery
Is equal in its period & value to Six Thousand Years.
For in this Period the Poet's Work is Done; and all the Great
Events of Time start forth & are conceiv'd in such a Period,
Within a Moment, a Pulsation of the Artery.   (*Milton*, pp. 27–8.)

Thus, according to Blake, not merely rest for wandering feet, but Eternity itself is to be found in the smallest clock's minutest beat; and the discovery of that eternal moment is the beginning of the transfiguration of the living man.

There is a Moment in each Day that Satan cannot find,
Nor can his Watch Fiends find it; but the Industrious find
This Moment, & it multiply: & when it once is found,
It renovates every Moment of the Day, if rightly placed.

(*Milton*, p. 35.)

Page 143. Though it is perfectly true that we do not know what life held in store for Alyosha Karamazov, there is no reason to be sceptical of the authenticity of the mystical vision with which Dostoevsky endowed him. I had no right to suggest that it was 'a doubtful beatitude'. The mystical vision was well known to Dostoevsky, who utters it even more remarkably in some of the speeches of Kirillov in *The Possessed* than in the famous vision of Alyosha.

Page 148. I leave the sentence as it was written; to me now it appears as making a mouth at the invisible event.